ETON & RUGBY FIVES

A complete handbook of practical advice, instruction and rules

By
David Egerton
&
John Armitage

INCORRECT AND CORRECT.

Top : EVERYONE IS WRONG HERE. " D " IS NOT UNDERNEATH THE BALL, AND IS ALMOST CERTAIN
TO MISS IT. " B " IS NOT LOOKING, WHILE " C " IS MANIFESTLY, AND REASONABLY, TERRIFIED.
Bottom : THIS IS BETTER. " D " IS NOW WELL UNDERNEATH THE BALL, THOUGH HE DOES NOT LOOK
AS IF HE INTENDS TO HIT IT VERY HARD. " C'S " POSITION IS GOOD, AS ALSO " B'S," THOUGH " B'S "
EYE SHOULD BE ON THE BALL.

" A " WON'T GET IT UP IF IT COMES OUT FROM THE PEPPER-BOX AFTER — — — — —. (BALL
OBSCURED BY GLOVE.) " B " WILL PROBABLY GET — — — — — UP, HOWEVER. " A " MIGHT GET
................., BUT IT IS UNLIKELY THAT HE COULD GET TO XXXXXXXXXX ; PERHAPS " B " COULD,
THOUGH.

CONTENTS

ILLUSTRATIONS

THE LAWS OF ETON FIVES

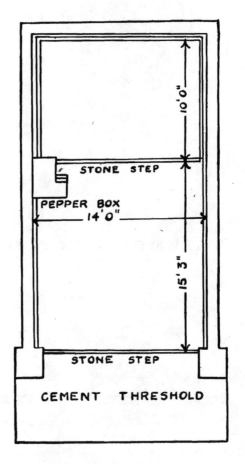

PLAN OF AN
ETON FIVES COURT

Fig. 1.

CHAPTER ONE

THE LAWS OF ETON FIVES

(Copyright of the Eton Fives Association)

DEFINITIONS

The court is enclosed on three sides and open at the back. The front wall is the wall facing the player, and the right-hand and left-hand walls are the walls on his right hand and left hand respectively.

The step is a shallow step dividing the court into two portions, an ' inner ' or ' upper ', and an ' outer ' or ' lower ' ' court ' or ' step '. The vertical face of the ' step ' does not reckon as part of the floor of the court.

The pepper-box is a buttress projecting from the left-hand wall. With the step, it encloses a small square portion of the floor called Dead Man's Hole.

The ' line ' is the lower angle of the ledge running across the front wall, at the height of 4 feet 6 inches.

A vertical line is marked on the front wall at a distance of 3 feet 8 inches from the right-hand wall.

LAWS

1. The ball must in every case be hit ' up ' ; i.e. it must be returned against the front wa on or above the line. Any ball which, after going ' up ', drops on the top of any of the walls or of the coping, or which hits any part of the roof, or which touches the ground first outside the court, or touches any person or object outside the court before the first bound, is ' out of court ', and *invariably* counts against the striker.

2. The ball must be fairly hit with a single blow of the hand or hands or wrist, and must not touch any other part of the striker's person under penalty of losing the stroke. It must not be caught, carried or held in any way, except to serve, or to stop a ball as provided in Laws 6 and 13.

N.B.—A ball taken with both hands or with a cupped hand may often be technically held, in which case the striker should declare a hold, and allow the point to go against him.

3. POSITION OF THE PLAYERS. The game is played by four persons, two against two. Thus if A and B, with first innings, play C and D, A, the server, must stand on the ' upper step '. C stands ready to return the service, and is said to be ' in holes '. B and D stand in the lower court, B having choice of position.

4. HOLES INNINGS. The choice of first innings shall be decided by tossing, &c. In the first innings of a game, if A goes in first, he is said to have ' holes innings ', and will be ' in holes ' when both A and B are put out. This applies only to the first innings : subsequently the player who has the second hand of an innings shall be ' in holes ', except as provided under Law 12. If in the first game, A has ' holes innings ' and C is ' in holes ', then in the second game C will have ' holes innings ' and A will be ' in holes '. In the third game B has ' holes innings ' and D is ' in holes '. In the fourth game D has ' holes innings ' and B is ' in holes ' In the fifth game, A has ' holes innings ' and C is ' in holes '.

5. THE SERVICE. The ball when served must hit first the front wall above the ' line ', and then the right-hand wall and must fall in the ' lower court ' The player ' in holes ' need not

return the first or any service until he gets one to his mind, and if he fails to return the service above the 'line', no stroke is counted. A service which goes 'out of court' carries no penalty.

6. THE FIRST CUT. The player 'in holes' must not return the service before the first bound. This return is called the first cut. He must return it so that it should hit either (1) first the right-hand wall and then the front wall above the 'line'; or (2) the front wall above the 'line' between the right-hand wall and the vertical line marked on the front wall. In both cases the ball may afterwards hit any wall or walls, and may fall anywhere on the 'upper' or 'lower step'. Only the player 'in holes' may return the service. A first cut which is up, but not in accordance with these conditions, is called a 'blackguard'. The player in holes or his partner may then touch or catch the ball before the first bound, and if this is done, no stroke is counted. If the ball is not touched or caught, it may be returned by either of the other two players at their option, and if it is not returned above the line, no stroke is counted.

7. THE RALLY. After the service and the first cut, the ball is returned alternately by either side. It may be returned by either of the partners before the second bound, and may or may not hit the side walls. A rally is lost to his side by the player who fails to return the ball above the 'line', or hits it 'out of court'.

8. LETS. A let may be claimed when a player is in any way prevented from returning, or impeded in his attempt to return the ball by one of the opposite side. A stroke which would have hit the front wall above the 'line', but is prevented from so doing by one of the opposite side, counts as a 'let'. A 'let' may not be claimed when a ball is hit 'out of court', nor when a player is impeded by bystanders. In all cases of doubt the Umpire's decision is final.

N.B.—If there is no Umpire, a claim is generally allowed.

9. LETS. If a ball while being returned, first strikes one of the opposite side, and then the front wall above the 'line', it counts as up; if it first strikes one of the same side, it counts as down, whether it goes up or not.

10. LETS. If a ball returned by A or B strike A or B after going up, before the second bound, it shall count as a 'let', whether or no C or D consider they could have returned it, if it had not hit A or B. C or D may however elect to return the ball and continue the rally. If not returned 'up', it counts as a let. If returned above the line a 'let' may not be claimed.

11. SCORING. The game consists of 15 points. Only the side which is 'up' may score points. When A is put 'out', B takes his place. When B is put 'out', the side is 'out', and their opponents go 'up', the player 'in holes' having first innings. The result of each rally, except in the case of a 'let', is either to add one to the score of the side which is 'up', or to put one of them 'out', as the case may be.

12. TWO DOWN. If C, 'in holes', loses one point to the opposite side, he is said to be 'one down'. If he loses a second point, he is said to be 'two down', and D takes his place. If D, in turn, loses two points, he is two down, and C is 'in holes' again, and so on until both A and B are put 'out'; provided that he who was 'two down' first is then the first to go 'up': but if, through inadvertence or otherwise he does not do so, the error cannot be corrected after the service has been returned. If the side 'in holes' loses a point by failing to return a ball out of Dead Man's Hole, it does not count as 'one down' against the player 'in holes'.

N.B.—For the purposes of this law, all balls which fall on the 'top step' belong to the player 'in holes', and also all balls on the 'lower step' which he attempts to return. The player 'in holes' cannot be two down at game ball.

13. If the player 'in holes' hits the first cut in such a way that it will probably fall 'out of court', he or his partner may, if they can, touch or catch the ball before it falls, provided that the player touching it has one or both feet on the floor of the court, or if he jumps for the purpose, alights on the floor of the court with the foot which first touches the ground. If the ball is caught, no stroke is counted; if only touched, the opposite player may, if he chooses, return the ball as in Law 10. If he fails to do so, no stroke is counted.

14. BLACKGUARD CUT. When the side which is 'up' reaches 14 points, the following Laws must be observed.

(1) The player serving must stand with one foot on the 'top step', and the other in the lower court', and he may not place both feet on the 'top step', until the player 'in holes' has

hit the ball. If he forgets to stand thus, and serves the ball with both feet on the ' top step ', the player ' in holes ' or his partner may try to *catch* the ball before it bounds. If they succeed in this, the *side* serving is out. If, however, the player serving or his partner manage to touch the ball first, or if it hits the ground before being touched, it counts neither way. A player may remind his partner of this Law.

(2) When the ball is properly served, the player ' in holes ' may return the ball against any part of the front wall above the ' line ', with or without hitting the side walls, and this is therefore called the blackguard cut. Law 6, except the first sentence, is suspended at this point of the game.

15. SETTING. If the players are 13 all, the game, as in rackets, may at the option of the side which is ' in holes ', be set to 5 or 3. If 14 all, to 3. Law 14 must then be observed at 4 and 2 respectively. At 17 all or 15 all in the first case, or 16 all in the second case, the game shall be decided by sudden death, Law 14 being observed by either side.

CHAPTER TWO

E T O N   F I V E S

BY DAVID EGERTON

'*DÉFENSE de Jouer à la Pélote.*' So runs a warning to the sacrilegious who wish to take exercise under the lee of Bayonne Cathedral. Pelota did not, I presume, have its origin amid the mossy drainpipes of an ecclesiastical atmosphere ; whereas Eton Fives most certainly did, and under a lenient ecclesiastical wing it has taken root, and developed to its present state. For many centuries the pastime of a few small boys, unofficial and unnoticed by the historian, it remains to-day a game for the few, its main enthusiasts being the schoolboy and the schoolmaster. That it has never caught the public eye and become popular must be ascribed to its complexity of rules, to its quaintness of court, and to the absolute necessity for four players to each game. (Let it be said at once that the singles game, as provided for in the rules published by A. C. Ainger in 1877, is not, and has not been, considered worth playing, and consequently no mention of any singles game is made in the 1931 revision of the rules. But it is quite possible that a satisfactory form of singles game may be evolved in the future.) Notwithstanding, very considerable progress has been made in recent years, and the number of available clubs and competitions is increasing rapidly.

Some form of Fives has existed from the very earliest days— amongst the Egyptians, Greeks and Romans alike. It is a far cry from these early games to the present-day Eton Fives. But Eton Fives is, like real Tennis and Pelota, a specialized development of older hand or racket games, and it is unnecessary for me to deal here with the history of small ball games at large.

The game of Eton Fives has evolved more by luck than by good management, owing to a series of happy accidents. To

12

hit a ball against a wall with the hand or a convenient piece of wood is instinctive to boys—no less at Eton than anywhere else. Fives must have been played in nearly all the bays of Upper Chapel. With one exception all these games were of the Rugby type, that is, games without a hazard, demanding only simple rules. Why the game we now call Eton Fives should have survived, we cannot tell. Let us put it down to the intrinsic superiority of any game which includes a hazard over any game which is not so fortunate.

All other Fives games have long been extinct at Eton, and this one alone has grown into a highly developed, if badly organized, game. But for centuries it existed at Eton quite unofficially, and had no importance in school life. It has been too insignificant to be mentioned by name in the College *Chronicle* or any other record previous to the late 'forties. But it is pleasant to assume that Thomas Gray, in his ' Ode on a Distant Prospect of Eton College ' was thinking of Fives in these lines :

> " What idle progeny succeed
> To chase the rolling circle's speed
> Or urge the flying ball ? "

Hazlitt, of course, was not an Etonian, and consequently, if interesting in his praise of Jack Cavanagh, he is ignorant of other forms of Fives, and therefore useless for our purposes. Apart from casual references in the *Eton College Chronicle* (after 1840) we have no bibliography to which to refer, save A. C. Ainger's chapter in the Tennis, Rackets and Fives Volume of the Badminton Library, and the late E. B. Noel's article in the *Encyclopædia Britannica*. (Noel was a Wykehamist.) Of these, the first is often irrelevant, and the latter is of necessity very compressed : both deal very summarily with the history of the game. The late Townsend Warner wrote an Essay on the game, together with some excellent hints for young players, the latter being reproduced with permission elsewhere in this book. In 1923 R. C. Clift wrote an excellent article, entitled ' How to Play Fives ', which was published in the Rackets and Fives handbook in Spaldings' Sports and Athletic Library. I must also mention a few interesting, if scattered, paragraphs in the late F. B. Wilson's book, *Sporting Pie*. This ends the bibliography, and leads to one of the main difficulties of Eton Fives : it must be learnt, and therefore it must be taught. Few of the great players have attained their greatness uncoached. Any fool can take up a Squash Racket and ball, enter a court,

and attain a reasonable state of proficiency enjoyably without
any tuition whatsoever. This is not so at Eton Fives, and unless
the beginner is well instructed from the start, it is likely that
he will soon tire, and give up the attempt through sheer bore-
dom and disgust. And it is this necessity for teaching, com-
bined with a lack both of precedent and of a competent ad-
visory and controlling body that has given rise to the many
and varied styles obtaining at the different schools ; for instance, the Etonian plays a slower and perhaps a more cunning
game than the Salopian ; the Harrovian volleys all he can ;
and the Carthusian hits very hard. Handbooks on cricket and
football appear with alarming frequency ; whether they raise
the standard of play is open to discussion, but they do help to
standardize the lines of teaching and the style of players.
While no one wants to see every school play Fives in the same
style—even supposing it were possible to prevail upon the innate
conservatism of the public schools to alter so important a part
of their mechanism as traditional style—yet I am certain that
each has much to learn from the others. More handbooks
would lead to more discussion, and discussion, I hope, to wider
views throughout. Though this is perhaps beside the point.

As we now have it, Eton Fives is a young game, but before
dealing with its modern history we must include, for those un-
acquainted with the original setting of the game, some description of the court which gave rise to our present game.
Jutting out from the north wall of the chapel is the main entrance. From it descends a flight of steps, running from east
to west, and having a low buttress near the lower end, to serve
as a hand rail. The pavement at the bottom of these steps
formed the back or outer court. The small buttress formed the
' Pepper-Box '. The upper court consisted of three walls : the
front wall, part of the north wall of the Chapel, and the side
walls, formed by two of the great buttresses, all of which tower
up above to a height of 70 or 80 feet—not that anything like the
whole height of these three walls could ever be used in the game.
The floor, which was a large step some 5 inches higher than
the floor of the outer court, was paved with flag-stones, some-
what unevenly laid, and sloping up at an angle to the front
wall. In the original court this angle was such as to make
standing rather uncomfortable, and the game, I should imagine,
difficult.

A convenient sloping ledge, at a height of 4 feet 6 inches,
formed the play-line, and another ledge about 2 feet from the

ground formed an additional hazard. Finally, the famous Dead Man's Hole is nothing more or less than one of the drains which served to take away surplus rain-water. Yet it is this feature of the court, and deservedly, which has caught the eye of such journalists as have lavished on the game a paragraph or two of sporting gossip in the evening papers. (Not a year passes but someone, during the week of the Public Schools Handicaps, announces his discovery of this weird new game !) For in Eton Fives, as in real Tennis, it is the accidents of the court which provide the true greatness of the game, and its undoubted superiority over all games in which no form of natural hazard exists.

A glance at the original court will show how difficult the game must have been, and would be now even given the great improvements made in modern equipment and balls. What type of ball was orginally used we do not know ; there are no records on this subject. The use of Fives gloves is a modern innovation, due in part to the hardness of the ball at present in use, and to the too-frequent damaging of fingers and knuckles against the many projections which go to make up the Eton Fives court. But lack of historical information compels me to make no attempt at a reconstruction of the game as played in, say, the seventeenth century.

The chapel court was in use until the first new courts were built in 1840. Certainly in 1825 the game flourished at a high standard, for Dr. E. H. Lyttelton's father played on it in that year, and " waxed eloquent on the skill required to return a ball from the far end of the ' off wall ', (lower step) while actually jumping off the steps "—i.e. the steps descending from the chapel entrance. In those days the difficulty seems to have been to return the ball at all, whereas in these times of fast covered courts, it is becoming increasingly difficult to kill the ball at all.

During the first half of the nineteenth century, the game gradually became popular at Eton, perhaps because there were no other organized games of any kind. The number of people who could play Fives in any one court was of course very limited, and certain houses built more or less exact replicas of the chapel court. One of these, called the Pig-Sty, from its close proximity to a shed in which some of these malodorous animals were housed, survived in the sixties, and part of it is still to be seen. These courts had no side walls to the lower court. (They resembled perhaps the early courts at Highgate, though these have side walls to the lower as well as the upper court.)

For the first great development in Eton Fives we are indebted to Dr. Hawtrey, sometime Headmaster of Eton. In 1840 he decided to build the first block of Eton Fives courts—four in number. He, or some other competent body, must have decided, with a stroke of genius, that, suitably adapted, a court modelled on the lines of the original court would prove a most ideal game for four people. For A. C. Ainger is wrong when he says that these four were an exact reproduction of the chapel court. We see immediately that the court—and thus the game —has been changed, not out of all recognition, but none the less to a considerable extent. The walls were built of sand-stone, so as to reproduce the effect of the chapel walls. But the distance between the front wall and the ' Pepper-Box ' was in-creased considerably, and the fall of the floor lessened by perhaps a half, two factors which made the game both easier and faster. Further, the side walls were made to project right out to the end of the back court instead of ceasing abruptly on a level with the ' Pepper-Box '. The ' Pepper-Box ' itself was increased in height, reduced in depth, and made to project farther out into the court. Alone the ' Dead Man's Hole ' and the ' coping ' on the front wall have remained unaltered.

It is, therefore, on Dr. Hawtrey's courts of 1840 that are founded all the courts of to-day, with very few alterations. But it is interesting to note that all the present courts at Eton, and all standard courts built elsewhere, are just 2 inches narrower, and 1 inch shorter than Dr. Hawtrey's courts. For, built as they were of sandstone, the surface decayed, and after a few years they had to be re-surfaced with cement, 1 inch being laid on all round. It is also improbable that the present rather dangerous step at the back of the court would exist but for the situation of Dr. Hawtrey's courts. They were built on gravel soil, but were subject to occasional flooding, and presumably in order to keep out the water, the courts were raised some 5 inches off the ground-level.

All these courts were naturally open to wind and rain (for it is only in the last twenty-five years that covered courts have been constructed) and all the floors fell away from the front wall towards the back of the court, in order to facilitate drying. This had obviously been the cause of the fall on the floor in the upper part of the chapel court, though the lower step had no fall on it.

Such were the courts which gave rise to the modern game of Eton Fives. About the development of the game during the next twenty or thirty years we know little, save that in 1847 eight more courts were added to the four courts of 1840.

Certainly until 1877 the rules were only such as existed by word of mouth, and it was many years before the game spread outside Eton itself. As usually happens in the case of a game which includes many hazards, the rules, for what they were worth, were exceedingly complicated, and necessitated, as they do still in part, a vocabulary of their own.—Words like ' Good 'Un ', for a ball hit out of court, take some explaining.

In 1877, A. C. Ainger, " in conjunction with several clear-headed friends " as he himself styles it, found it incumbent upon himself to draw up and publish the *Rules of the Game of Fives as Played at Eton*. And these rules have sufficed for succeeding generations of Fives-Players until the publication of the Laws (Note the Change !) of Eton Fives by the committee of the Eton Fives Association in March, 1931. A. C. Ainger's rules, excellent in their way, left much to the imagination and good nature of the players concerned, and probably he himself intended that they should be revised within a few years of their first publication. By 1931 they were found to be out of date in many points.

The new laws were called laws at the instance of the late F. B. Wilson, who insisted, and rightly, that ' one of the great games ' must have laws—rules are left to the more childish modern games. These new laws themselves are not by any means perfect, and will doubtless come up for revision again during the course of the next two or three years. But it must be owned that they have cleared up a large number of difficulties which existed previously, and further, they have one great advantage over A. C. Ainger's rules : they have practically eliminated ' local rules ', once the bugbear (I have heard it called delight) of all who play Eton Fives on other than their own home courts. When the laws were being compiled, all the public schools were consulted, and invited to send in the peculiarities private to their own courts. In many cases it was discovered that the differences of rules, or of interpretation of Ainger's rules, entirely altered the complexion of the game.

At the time which we have been considering, Eton possessed the only courts in the world, but at Eton the game was fast increasing in standard and popularity, so much so that the number of courts was not sufficient for the needs of the school.

B

In 1870, A. C. Ainger with characteristic energy persuaded Old Etonians to subscribe sufficient money to build twelve new courts, and then by a happy inspiration ' saddled each house with the task of building a court for itself '. With experience successive courts improved rapidly in structure, and many of these early courts are still in use, and should continue to serve their purpose for years to come.

After 1870 the game spread rapidly. Many public schools, notably Harrow (c. 1870), Charterhouse, Highgate, and West-minster (1886), built courts. In most cases Old Etonians resident as Head- or Assistant-Masters were responsible for the building of these courts, but it was long before the game became popular. At Cambridge over a dozen courts were built be-tween 1890 and 1900, and a large number of open courts were also to be found in country houses all over England. For the most part, however, these courts only resembled the true Eton Courts very haphazardly : in actual dimensions and angles there were large divergences from the accurate. Those who built courts, did not, it seems, realize the great differences bound to arise out of the smallest alterations in the size of the court. The obvious conclusion is that the speed and standard of play were not so high as is the case to-day. In truth it must be stated that one of the chief objections to Eton Fives has always lain in the wide variations to be found in different Eton Fives courts. To-day it is considered important to have all courts uniform, and accurate drawings and specifications are now available for all who wish to build Eton Fives courts.

At most schools the game did not prosper and was not con-sidered worthy of any outside matches until 1885. In this year E. M. Butler, captain of Fives at Harrow, received a challenge from Freeman Thomas (now Lord Willingdon, Viceroy of India, one of the greatest players of all time), then Keeper of Fives at Eton, to an Eton Fives match, one pair aside. Natur-ally Butler and his partner, B. R. Warren, were no match for the Etonians. But though Harrow in general paid little or no attention to this visit of the Etonians, yet it undoubtedly gave birth to a new keenness, and entirely revised the ideas of the game then in force at Harrow. For, having been shown the way Fives was played at Eton, the standard of Harrow's play started to rise very rapidly. The date February 12, 1885, is a very important stepping-stone in the history of Eton Fives. A tradition started on that day still exists—for Eton still plays all its more important Fives matches one pair aside.

Soon afterwards matches began to be played among such schools as Charterhouse and Uppingham. No school, however, could hold a candle to Eton until the late G. Townsend Warner returned to Harrow as an assistant master in 1891, and took on the teaching of Fives. Townsend Warner learnt his Fives at Cambridge, where he was a contemporary of E. M. Butler and Lord Willingdon. From Lord Willingdon both Warner and Butler learnt much, and on returning to Harrow they imparted all they knew to their pupils. The result was a great step forward in Harrow Fives. In 1900 the late F. B. Wilson and R. H. Crake defeated Eton both at home and away for the first time. In 1904, 1905, 1906, E. H. Crake (brother of R. H.) and R. E. Eiloart beat Eton both at home and away with the loss of only 3 games in six matches—a remarkable feat. Even so, this pair at their best were never able to extend Townsend Warner and Butler. Indeed, this pair was only once beaten during the whole of their match-playing career as Harrow masters, and that once by a pair of Charterhouse masters.

It is, then, owing to A. C. Ainger at Eton, and both Townsend Warner and E. M. Butler at Harrow, that the standard reached a very high peak at both these schools. Amongst other schools where the game was well played were Shrewsbury, Charterhouse, Westminster, Highgate and Uppingham. And later there were many others such as Repton, where it was introduced by the late Lionel Ford, then Headmaster, and the City of London School. Even Rugby had two or three courts, but the game never caught on there. But between 1890 and 1900 Eton Fives was at the height of its popularity and prosperity.

And so the game flourished until the outbreak of the Great War. But except for a few Old Etonian enthusiasts who built themselves courts at their country houses, Eton Fives was confined for the most part to schoolboys and schoolmasters ; whereas it should make a most excellent form of exercise for the middle-aged. In London the only court to be found outside the schools was in the open at Queen's Club—and this was occupied all too rarely. Oxford contained but a single court, which belonged to Merton College, and many of the Cambridge courts were gradually falling into decay. Lord Kinnaird, F. B. Wilson, and Ralph Straus had often played when they were up, but after their day, it was no longer fashionable.

The War did its best to kill Eton Fives, notwithstanding a

much-used court at St. Mary's Hospital at Sidcup in Kent.
After the War, Fives was in a sorry state. During the War the
public schools had had little time to play Fives, and few active
pre-war players remained. Its revival, however, was rapid, and
the next few years showed the birth of a new and keener set of
Fives players, people who were not content to have finished
their Fives-playing days when they left school. The formation of
Old Boys' Fives clubs did much to satisfy their needs. Indeed,
the greater part of the Eton Fives played outside the schools
to-day is played by the Old Boys' clubs. Much gratitude is
due to W. E. Gerrish, who started and ran the Old Westminsters
Fives Club for many years, and also to J. G. King, the moving
spirit of the Old Etonian Fives Association. Both clubs played
matches far and wide, and the Old Westminsters even sent sides
touring all the schools and Fives courts to be found in the
country, all of which gave a most useful start to the revival of
the game.

Old boys of other Eton Fives playing schools soon followed
suit and formed similar Fives clubs. To-day there are at least
a dozen clubs of this kind.

Much has also been done to promote competitions. In 1924
Lord Kinnaird gave a challenge cup to be competed for by the
Old Boys' Fives clubs, and though it lapsed for a couple of years
after its inception, the building of the covered Fives court at
Queen's Club in 1927 set it well on its feet once more. The
number of entries increases practically every year. In 1931 the
Kinnaird Cup regulations were revised and the title of the
competition was altered to ' Amateur Championship for the
Kinnaird Cup ', thus giving it a larger showing of importance.

Public Schools Handicaps have taken place at Queen's Club
since 1929, and the improvement in the standard of play has
been consistent and noteworthy.

In 1932 a new competition, called the ' Queen's Club Competition ', and run on the lines of the Bath Club Cup at Squash
Rackets, was started between the Old Boys' clubs. While the
need for such a competition was obvious, the success of it still
remains to be seen.

Such briefly is the history of Eton Fives. Though much has
been done since the War to set it in its proper position amongst
other ball games, equally much remains to be done. If the
present plans for the improvement of courts and conditions of
play are successful, then the game should enter on a period of
prosperity hitherto unforeseen.

CHAPTER THREE

ETON FIVES (continued)

BY DAVID EGERTON

A BRIEF description of the game of Eton Fives is likely to leave a layman reader in the same kind of bewilderment experienced by the casual visitor to the dedans of a real Tennis court. Rhyme and Reason, at first sight, seem complete strangers to the laws of both games, and it is highly probable that no one will make any start towards understanding either game until he enters the court and tries for himself. It shall be my endeavour, then, rather to attempt to help the eager beginner, if such a one exists, than to give a motion-picture account to the middle-aged arm-chaired sportsman.

To understand the setting and form of the game, it is only necessary to turn to the *Laws of Eton Fives* (see page 9). Read first the Definitions, and then the first four laws of Eton Fives, for in these are to be found the first essentials for the playing of the game. After a careful study, the reader will gather roughly the shape of the court ; the fact that four players are required ; how these players stand ; and who starts. The use of A and B, partners, opposing C and D, partners, may prove confusing to some in the actual telling. To find a more simple way of designating the players and their relative and respective positions is difficult.

Assuming that the reader has digested the Laws and Definitions as requested, making use also of the plan of the court to be found on page 8, we will consider him ready to watch his first game of Eton Fives, or, if need be, to take the place of A, B, C, or D.

Standing about behind the back of the court are the four players, taking off surplus apparel before starting to knock up. And here we must digress a moment in order to discuss the question of dress and equipment. Dress is simple : the only necessity is that whatever is worn should leave both waist and arms and legs the most complete freedom of movement. Any restrictions caused by a player's dress are likely to injure his play, and may obstruct his opponents. Therefore, if trousers are worn, they should neither be too tight in the seat, nor too long in the leg ; for a restriction in the girth is enough to prevent a player bending either fast enough or far enough (Eton Fives is essentially a game of extremes : one second the player is, so to speak, picking the ball off his toes, and the next he has to jump in order to reach a volley). Trousers, if too long, are apt to catch underneath the shoes and trip the player up. Shirt-sleeves should not be permitted to flap in the breeze, as not only are opponents distracted thereby, but sometimes they are even obstructed in their endeavour to return the ball, thus causing a let, as provided for in Laws 8 and 9. Shoes should be both as light and as strong as possible, with a sole of crêpe or other strong rubber compound—ordinary rubber wears out in a very short time on the rough floors of the average Fives court. Care should be taken to see that the shoe-laces are well tied, for a loose lace may cause a player to fall and twist his ankle.

Finally, and most important, the gloves : most players use gloves made of leather, of which the fingers and the palm are thinly and evenly padded, in order to prevent bruised hands. It often happens that the padding provided is not sufficient. In such cases it is usual to wear a pair of ' inners ', either ordinary woollen or chamois-leather gloves. The essential is to have gloves which, while not being so thin as to let the hand be damaged, yet give complete control over placing and ' cut '. It is quite possible that inners may interfere with the control over the ball—players whose gloves are too thickly padded invariably control the ball badly—but if the hands are subject to continual bruising, there is naturally no alternative but to wear additional protection. Bruised hands are, however, quite unnecessary if sufficient care is taken.

No hard hitting should be indulged in until the hands are thoroughly warm. To start with warm hands and gloves may mean a vital six or seven points while the other side is warming up, and many players make a point of thoroughly warming their gloves and hands in front of a fire, or the latter by soaking them in hot water, before entering a Fives court.

If one hand becomes slightly bruised, it should be rested as

THE SERVICE.

Top: "A" IS JUST GOING TO SERVE TO "D" FOR BLACKGUARD CUT AT GAME BALL. "A'S" SERVICE WOULD BE IMPROVED IF HE WERE TO SERVE FROM NEARER THE MIDDLE OF THE COURT, BUT THEN POSSIBLY HE WOULD BE IN "D'S" WAY. (BALL IS IN "A'S" HAND.)

Centre: "D" THROWING UP SERVICE LEFT-HANDED. NOTICE POSITION WELL OUT INTO THE MIDDLE OF THE COURT. (BALL IN "D'S" HAND.)

Bottom: "C" BOWLING A SERVICE. NOTICE HIS GOOD BALANCE. THIS SHOULD BE A GOOD SERVICE. (BALL IN "C'S" HAND.)

far as possible, by hitting more with the undamaged hand. But it is noteworthy that the truly ambidextrous player very rarely hurts either hand seriously, as such damage almost always results from over-strenuous use of the hand in question. Should a hand be badly bruised, it is essential to rest it for days, and even weeks, until it has completely ceased hurting, otherwise the particular part damaged will continue to give pain throughout the whole season, if not permanently. A small piece of rubber inserted between the glove and the injured portion of the hand often serves to protect a bruise ; others make use of ' plasticine ', putty, and raw beef, each of which is excellent in its way.

To return to the game : now the first four laws have dealt primarily with the theory of most small-ball games—that the ball shall be returned ' up ', and that it shall be hit with a single blow of the implement concerned, in this case the ' hand or hands or wrist '. This is in the nature of elementary and general information : they have also stated where the several players shall take up their positions, and how the game shall begin. These laws are, so to speak, fundamental and should require little or no explaining.

Before returning later to discuss the laws, points of style and various other matters, we will pass to a short description of a game of Eton Fives, for the benefit of our onlooker.

Each game is divided into so many ' rallies ', the object of each rally being either to score a point oneself, or, by preventing one's opponents from scoring, to put one's own side into such a position that it shall be able to score a point in the next rally, if it is fortunate or skilful enough to win that one also. The rally may be subdivided, for the sake of clearness, into three parts : (1) the service, which at no time can have any effect on the score of the game ; (2) the first cut ; and (3) all play following the first cut.

The player who is about to serve, here called A, is ' in '. He alone of the four players stands on the ' upper step ' before and during the service. The server's partner, B, should stand on the right-hand side of the court, near the outer step. (B has the right to stand on whichever side he pleases, but except in certain cases which will be explained later, as a general rule he stands on the right-hand side of the court.) C, who is ' in holes ', should stand just below the top step, in the centre of the court. He must be ready to return the service by means of the first cut. D, his partner, should stand at the back of the court, on whichever side of the court B is not standing. Thus :

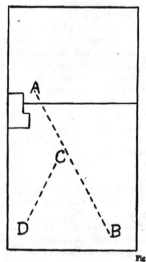

Fig. 2.

It will be seen that the four players form a Lambda, λ.

When A serves the ball (see Law 5) to C's liking, then C returns it by means of the first cut (see Law 6). He may return it either to A or B, or both may be forced to alter their positions considerably in their efforts to retrieve the ball. Thereafter the ball must be returned up alternately by either side. The side which first fails to return the ball above the line is deemed to have lost the rally, and thereby loses either a hand, or a point (see Law 11). While no point can be won or lost by the service, the first cut is of great importance, as a first cut which defeats the ' in ' side, ends the rally as described above. Even in first-class fives, quite a third of the first cuts which are up, win the rally outright.

When the rally has survived the taking of the first cut—which is certainly the most difficult part of Eton Fives—it may continue for any number of strokes, 40 or 50 strokes being not uncommon, while rallies of 70 and 80 strokes have been recorded.

As the laws state emphatically, " the result of each rally

THE SERVICE AND FIRST CUT.

Top : " B'S " SERVICE SHOULD BE GOOD. " D " OUGHT TO BE WATCHING THE BALL. " C " LOOKS WIDE AWAKE AND SHOULD STOP A "GOOD 'UN."

Bottom : " D'S " FIRST CUT WILL PROBABLY NOT GO UP, BUT IN ANY CASE IT WOULD NOT BE GOOD AS HE HAS IMPARTED NO CUT TO THE BALL, AND HIS LEFT HAND IS NOT FAR ENOUGH FORWARD.

(except in the case of a let) is either to add one point to the score of the side which is up, or to put one of them out, as the case may be ". Thus if A is serving, should A and B win the rally, their side gains a point, and A serves again, and for each successive rally, until C and D make a winning stroke. This puts A ' out ', and B takes his place as server, being called the second hand of the innings. When B is put out, both hands are said to be out. C now becomes the server, as first hand of the innings, and B is ' in holes '. (Note that in the first innings of a game, known as Holes Innings, A, and not B, will be ' in holes ' when both A and B have been put out.) B, unless he is two down (see Law 12), remains ' in holes ' until both C and D are put out. D then takes his place ' in holes,' and B, now the server, goes up and is the first hand of the new innings.

And so the rally and subsequent rallies proceed until one side or other has reached 14 points. When a side reaches 14 points, it is said to have reached game ball, and appears to be within, as we might say, marching distance of its goal. It is here that the true struggle begins, for, *pour encourager les autres*, the laws here go, to the beginner's way of thinking, completely mad, and start supporting the losing side for all they are worth. The potential losers are now, as it seems, entitled to murder the would-be winners, as will be seen from a study of Law 14, parts one and two. Not content with giving the losers every chance to win a point off an ideal service, it is now ordered that the server shall stand in the most awkward of positions, and the player ' in holes ' is further entitled to hit the ball wheresoever he pleases, provided that in its crazy career it strikes the front wall above the ' line '. Supposing A to be in the enviable position of being up when his side has 14 points to its credit, then A is forced to leave his corner, stand with one foot (in the grave ?) in the upper court, and the other in the lower court (which foot on which step is fortunately not provided for in the laws, and is left to the choice and discretion of the server). A must then proceed to pitch and bounce the ball where and how C demands (in accordance with Law 5) ; nor may A move from his awkward position until C has hit the ball as outlined above. Such a first cut is easily hit so as to be difficult to take, and indeed is often the cause of a much-delayed victory, or a victory turned into defeat. I can remember more than once leading by 14 points to 6 in a game, and then having lost it, partly through over-confidence, and partly owing to the excellent first cuts of my opponents. This Blackguard cut,

as it is called, is designed to defeat the over-confident, and is one
of the most admirable features of the Eton game. For in Eton
Fives, doubly more than in any other game, the match is never
lost until the other side has actually won, and victory is made
ten times more difficult owing to this singularity of the game.

Should both sides reach 13 all or 14 all, the game, as in
Rackets, is set, to 3 or 5 in the first case (at the option of the
side which is ' in holes '), and to 3 in the second case. Here
game ball and its accompanying rites take place at 2 or 4,
according as 3 or 5 has been set. Should both sides reach 2 or
4, the game is not re-set, both sides being Game Ball when
' up ', until one side or the other wins the necessary point.

The usual length of a single game is in the neighbourhood
of twenty minutes, though it is not unusual for a hard-fought
game to last three-quarters of an hour. A match consists of
the best of 3 or 5 games ; in the case of competitions, usually the
best of 5 games. A long match often lasts nearly two hours,
sometimes even longer.

The reader will probably gather from the last few paragraphs
that Eton Fives consists of a Service, a First Cut, an occasional
Rally, and an interminable Game Ball. This, of course, is not
so, but it is, I think, these features which are the most striking
to the onlooker. In a good match, however, the rallies are
long, often apparently unending, but following as they do in
a well-ordered series, it is not necessary to give a complete description of all that goes to make up the cycle of shots and
positions which occur during the course of the game.

Even so, our cart has beaten our horse. Let us now return
to the beginning of Fives, and discuss some of the more important features of the game. Every game of Fives must begin
with the service, and it is fitting that we should start by considering this most important factor of the game.

The late F. B. Wilson, leaning over the gallery of the court
at Queen's Club, and seeing someone serving carelessly, would
remark : " Ah ! Eton would never have served that sort of stuff
when I used to play them as a boy ! " Which being inter-
preted is his own modest way of saying : " —— help Harrow if
they served like that against Eton when I was captain of Fives."
And surely he was quite correct in attaching supreme importance to the service. It is an integral part of the spirit of the
game, and (with Rugby Fives of course) must be the only
instance in any modern game of a player deliberately giving his
opponent the best possible chance of defeating him. Too much

Plates **VI** & **VII**

FIRST CUT.

Top : THIS IS A BETTER ONE. GOOD FOLLOW THROUGH BY " D." THE POSITIONS OF THE OTHER THREE PLAYERS ARE ALL GOOD.

Bottom : " B " HAS GOT THIS FIRST CUT UP. NOTICE " D " UP ON TOP STEP READY TO KILL " B'S " RETURN IF A POOR ONE.

stress cannot possibly be laid on the importance of giving a good service. A good service, of course, means a service to the liking of the player 'in holes'. Now the player 'in holes' may, in strict accordance with his rights, demand a ball which bounces sideways, or which breaks backwards, and one cannot hope to cater for the eccentricities of madmen such as these. Such cases will hardly ever arise, it is to be hoped. The normal service expected is one which bounces to shoulder height, and which falls 'true', that is, without breaking. This is the essence of any good service, and can be obtained without trouble after a very little practice.

Advancing from the pepper-box into the middle of the court, the server should lob, throw, or bowl the ball high up on to the front wall so that it hits also the right-hand wall near to the top. It should bounce just below, but as near as possible to the foot of the top step, about 2 or 3 feet from the right-hand wall. Great care should be taken that no spin is imparted to the ball when thrown, or the service will break badly when it bounces, and a service which breaks at all is very difficult to hit satisfactorily. Left-handers will have to advance farther into the centre of the court than right-handers, for otherwise their service will fall awkwardly and break.

The server need not be afraid that the first cut will catch him out of position when it comes, for he has ample time to retreat and take up his chosen position, if he starts back as soon as he has thrown the ball.

Most players like the service to bounce as high as possible, but some will want it either near to the right-hand wall, or in the centre of the court, for which the server must serve from nearer the centre of the court or farther back towards the pepper-box, as the case may be. At all times, however, the server should try to send the best service within his power, remembering that the player 'in holes' need not, as the law says, "take the first or any service until he gets one to his mind". Nor should the server take advantage of this to serve continually badly, under the impression that he will wear down his opponent into hitting a weak first cut. Some years ago a master at Eton, who used to play regularly, was accustomed, when playing with a bad server, to refuse perhaps a dozen services in succession, good and bad alike. Then all of a sudden he would take one, when least expected, and hit it very hard indeed, regardless of how it pitched for him ; the result was nearly always an 'ace'.

Of recent years the serving in many of the public schools has
been deplorable, and, bearing in mind the discourtesy of a bad
service, it is to be hoped that greater care will be taken over
this exceedingly important feature of the game.

After the service it is natural to consider the first cut, the
most important stroke in Eton Fives. He who knows how to
vary his first cuts in pace and direction can often stave off defeat
from players considerably better than himself, and can start
each rally in a position of attack. Looking at Law 6, we find
that two forms of first cut are permitted, that which hits first
the right-hand wall and then the front wall above the line ;
and that which hits the front wall above the line between the
right-hand angle and the blackguard line, 3 feet 8 inches to the
left. (A cut which hits the front wall to the left of the blackguard line is called a blackguard, and may or may not be
returned by the server or his partner at their discretion.)
The first of these is the more usual. The main essentials of this
form of first cut are that it should be hit as low above the line
as possible, and that it should drop as near to the feet of the
server as possible. To obtain this, the ball must be ' cut ' with
a downward movement of a loose wrist at the moment of im-
pact. Now in Eton Fives, as in all other ball games, the one
unbreakable rule is : Keep your eye on the ball. " The front
wall never moves : the ball does." That this particular remark was not made about Eton Fives does not matter, it holds
good throughout. A player soon knows by heart the positions
of the various features of the court, and it is by these rather
than by the positions of his opponents that he should direct his
strokes. I do not mean that he should disregard his opponents'
positions : far from it, for many points can be won by making
them run so fast and so far that finally they are completely
unable to reach a shot. A good player senses his opponents'
positions almost out of the back of his head. The ball demands
the maximum of concentration which can be spared for it, and
other things must starve for this to be satisfied.

The second most important factor in Eton Fives is the position
of the feet. Nobody in his right mind attempts to throw or
bowl off the wrong foot ; and so in Eton Fives it is equally
essential to have the feet in the correct position so that the
weight of the body may be transferred forwards at the exact
moment of striking the ball. To a certain extent it is true that
where the eye goes, the feet follow automatically, i.e. they range
themselves in the correct order and position. That footwork is

automatic in the born Fives player is an undoubted fact, but
others would do well to spare a larger amount of trouble on its
perfection.   No definite rules can be laid down to say how
perfect footwork in Fives can be attained, for the game moves
too fast, and moreover sometimes circumstances force even the
most expert players into the awkward predicament of having
to play a shot off the wrong foot.   Such a stroke is bound to
lack accuracy, and in all probability pace as well.   The only
hard-and-fast rule for the beginner is to keep well forward on
the toes, and to aim to have the opposite foot forward to the
hand with which he is hitting.   There is a very short interval
between the ball leaving the wall, and its arrival within striking
distance, and the good player anticipates the direction of his
opponent's return even before he has made the stroke.   This
anticipation is largely a question of experience, and the good
player knows that his own previous shot can only permit of
a certain number of alternative returns, which are further
diminished by the positions of his opponents.   In order the
quicker to be able to make a sudden change if it should be
necessary, he remains always on the tips of his toes.

And while on the subject of essentials, it will be well to deal
with the two which remain—equal use of both hands, and
looseness of wrist.   Unfortunately or fortunately, few of us are
born with the ability to hit a Fives ball equally' hard and
accurately with either hand.   If we were—and here perhaps I
may speak also for Rugby Fives—then I venture to say that the
standard of both games would be considerably higher than it is.
The large majority of us are born with overwhelming right
hands, while our left hands appear to suffer from a form of
paralysis.   Now a game in which the left hand is more necessary would be hard to find ; the very shape of the court gives
a constant stream of balls to the left hand, as many ' right-
hand-only ' players have found to their cost.   To retrieve balls
from the pepper-box with the right hand is twice as difficult as
with the left hand.   That a weak left hand or right hand can
be greatly improved by never seeking to take a ball, ' volley or
first hop ' with the uncorrect hand, is true, but it is only by
constant practice, alone in a court, that a weak hand can be
made really strong.   Indeed, this form of practice is strongly to
be recommended throughout.

Most of the failure to hit with a weak hand can be attributed
to faulty footwork, for whereas the feet, as I have said, automatically place themselves correctly when the ball is going to

be hit by a player's natural hand, yet when it is a question of
using his useless hand, his feet are usually to be found completely out of position.

Finally the loose wrist : except in one or two special strokes
to be outlined later on, every hit should be made with a loose
wrist, and more especially so if the stroke is to be played from
above the height of the elbow. A stiff wrist will cause the ball
to travel very slowly, and to rise after it hits the front wall,
either presenting an easy volley to the opposing side, or coming
to earth far out of court. Having wandered farther than may
seem necessary, we must return to the muttons in question, the
first cut. It was the feet or the eye which made me wander.
Seeing the importance of this errant pair, the reader will have
to pardon the long and tedious interruption.

There are two main types of first cut. Of these the more
important is that which hits first the right-hand wall and then
the front wall. The greatest error made by the beginner is his
overpowering desire to hit every first cut hard enough to beat
the cover off the ball. Indeed this fault is not confined to the
beginner, and while more experienced players should know
better, is undoubtedly the cause of countless hands bruised unnecessarily each year. Let it suffice to say that, unless direction
and cut are correctly applied, the harder a first cut is hit, the
easier it is to take. But a hard right-handed first cut, well
placed, with plenty of ' cut ' on it, and hit as near to the angle
as possible, will be difficult to take. This ' cut ' is obtained by
drawing the wrist downwards sharply as the hand hits the ball.
If sufficient ' cut ' is applied to the ball, it will drop rapidly,
and should reach the ground not far distant from the server's
toes, or the Dead Man's Hole. (In a very fast or a ' sweating '
court it will often miss the pepper-box altogether, after the
manner of the left-hand first cut described later on. For these
B should be on the *left*-hand side of the lower court), and in
any case it will be difficult to return. In order to get pace
on the ball in this stroke, it is necessary to use not only the
wrist and the arm, but also the whole weight of the body, by
transferring the mass from the back foot, that is to say, the foot
on the same side as the hand with which the stroke is made,
to the forward foot, during the production of the shot. It is
a question of accurate timing, a steady eye, and a loose wrist
and shoulder. The whole arm and body should follow right
through with the completion of the stroke. The end of this or
any other first cut should coincide with the player ' in holes '

IN THE PEPPER-BOX.

Top: "A" HAS MADE A BAD STROKE, AND IS ABOUT TO SUFFER FOR IT, FOR "D", HUNGRY AS A TIGER, WILL KILL IT. "A" BEING BADLY OUT OF POSITION WILL PROBABLY RECEIVE THE BALL FAST AND TRUE IN HIS STOMACH.

Bottom: "A" RETRIEVING BALL IN PEPPER-BOX. HOW IT GOT THERE IS A MYSTERY, AS NEITHER "C" NOR "D" LOOK AS IF THEY COULD HAVE HIT IT THERE. "A" WILL MAKE A BAD STROKE AS HIS EYE IS NOT ON THE BALL.

following his stroke up on to the top step, for two reasons :
(1) His cut may go round all three walls, and return again to
the middle of the court, in which case he must on no account
be in a position to obstruct his opponent's return ; and (2) a
large number of points can be obtained in every game by volleying, if not killing ' dead ', soft returns put up by the server in
his mistaken efforts to return the ball out of the reach of the
player ' in holes ' or his partner. Only under exceptional
circumstances should this rule be broken.

To perfect this shot requires constant practice, and even when
perfected, it should not be used unchanged throughout an
entire game, for it is exceedingly tiring and in the later stages
of the game it is apt to become loose in its direction. Moreover,
the other side is apt to learn how to deal with any one stroke
which is being continually plastered at them. Therefore the
first cut should constantly be varied, and the cunning player
will find endless alternatives open to him ; a most effective
stroke is that which, played hard against the front wall, grazes
the right-hand wall all the way down the court. It should
bounce about 2 feet from the back step. If accurately hit, it
will often touch the brick projection of the back pillar, and is
usually untakeable. In any case, if it hugs the wall all the way
down it is always difficult to take, and endangers an opponent's
fingers, and may often catch him completely unawares. A first
cut hit in exactly the same direction, but very gently so that it
bounces on the top step, is often the cause of both the server and
his partner getting out of position, and will make a useful open-
ing for the player ' in holes ' to make a winning volley.

Finally, perhaps most useful of all, is the first cut which, hit
gently and with plenty of cut on it, strikes first the right-hand
wall *some distance away* from the angle, then the front wall, and
finally falls low down and awkwardly to the left hand of the
server. This cut is most effective, for three reasons : (1) it can
be made without great physical effort, and is useful when one is
tired ; (2) it confuses the server and his partner because (3) it
may bounce in at least three different directions, assuming that
it is too low for the server to volley easily. It will either hit
the left-hand wall about 2 inches above the level of the floor,
a difficult shot to retrieve, as the bounce keeps low ; or it may
bounce before it hits the left-hand wall, and at its first bounce pass
into the pepper-box, or come out behind the server's back ; or it
may hit the pepper-box first bounce and then hit the left-hand
wall. Thus it is always a useful method of troubling opponents.

As a general rule a first cut which is hit hard round all three walls is useless. The server, if able to volley with his left hand, will reach and perhaps kill it before it touches the left-hand wall ; or he will leave it to come round to his partner, for whom it is always an easy shot.

The shape of an Eton Fives court particularly benefits the left-hander—not least in the first cut. Naturally all the strokes here described for the right-hander are equally useful for the left-hander—with a difference, for the spin imparted by a left-handed first cut is in every case exactly opposite to that of a right-handed shot, and consequently the first cut of a left-hander will prove confusing to the server and his partner. The hard first cut of a left-hander, which hits first the right-hand wall and then the front wall, is peculiarly effective, and has a habit of making straight for the Dead Man's Hole, or missing the pepper-box completely, when it will give the server's partner a difficult return from the back of the court. (To take this cut the server's partner should stand on the *left*-hand side of the lower court.)

To be able to ' cut ' equally well with both hands should be the aim of every player. Unfortunately it is given to few, though much can be effected by diligent practice. Besides being able to rest one hand or the other in case of emergency, the ambidextrous player almost doubles the variety of first cut at his command.

If one player of a four is able to cut with both hands, when he is ' in holes ', the server's partner should say to the server ' Right Hand ' or ' Left Hand ' according to the hand which the player ' in holes ' is preparing to use. This will enable the server the more easily to anticipate the probable direction of the first cut.

The partner of the player ' in holes ' should constantly be on the look-out for the stray first cut which occasionally will hit the upper part of the ledge which forms the play-line ; for such strokes are very often bad luck, and are likely to land out of court. It is the duty to prevent this happening, by " touching or catching the ball " (see Law 13), and thus to save a point for his side.

I cannot here pretend to give a comprehensive list of all the first cuts open to the player who uses his head. The variety is endless, and the repertoire can be, and is, continually expanded as experience grows.

CHAPTER FOUR

E T O N   F I V E S (*continued*)

BY DAVID EGERTON

NO less important than the first cut itself is the taking of it, which devolves upon the server or his partner. No definite rules can be laid down as to where the server shall stand in order to return the first cut ; it is largely a question of experience and must be decided by each player for himself : moreover, both the court and the player ' in holes ' must be taken into consideration. In a very fast or a sweating court, the first cut will tend to miss the pepper-box altogether, in which case the server, if he is to attempt to take these first cuts, must advance out well into the middle of the court, rather than occupy his usual position in or near the pepper-box. Under normal conditions to receive a right-handed first cut, the server should stand well forward on his toes about 2 feet out diagonally from the pepper-box and left-hand wall. He should mark where and how his service pitches, and must immediately transfer his eye and undivided attention diagonally across the court to the right-hand angle. Failure to observe this will infallibly cause the server to miss the first cut when it does arrive. (Some players possessed of a very quick eye find it possible and better to watch the ball right off the hand of the player ' in holes ', following it round until it reaches their own hand in due and short course. For the most part this is not to be recommended.)

The first cut should always be volleyed if high enough ; this will be difficult, if not impossible, when the first cut lands at or near the server's feet. In such cases the server may use the half-volley, always a defensive stroke, or, if he is quick enough, he may turn round and take the ball first bounce from the pepper-box. In any case the return of first cut, more especially if a volley is made, should be hit with one hand and not with two hands. Of recent years at certain public schools a habit has arisen of taking the first cut with two hands ; this is entirely wrong, as it leads to the ball

C

being pushed, rather than 'fairly hit with a single blow'.
Two hands, though sanctioned by the laws, should only be
used in very rare instances.

Many have advocated that the server, immediately after
throwing up the service, should crouch in the pepper-box,
with the knees fully bent, in order to be able to volley or
half-volley a good first cut. There are two objections to this
position : (1) Should a first cut come shoulder high, or higher,
only a defensive stroke can be played, for it is impossible to
hit an overhead shot hard when crouching down. (2) If for
any reason the server wishes to move quickly, he must first
waste a vital moment in getting up to normal posture. It is
much easier to bend down quickly than to get up from a
crouch in a hurry, and normally there is plenty of time to
stoop when necessary.

The main fault to avoid when taking the first cut is ' snatch-
ing ' at the ball. Never be in too great a hurry to make the
stroke. So many are the ledges and angles of an Eton Fives
court that a second attempt is often possible if the first attempt
has hit nothing but air !

Care should be taken to see that the return does not give
the player ' in holes ' an easy volley—for if he is a good player,
he will be waiting on the step for a chance of a smash. Try
and make an ' offensive ' stroke, either a lob which just, and
only just, clears the top of the pepper-box, or a low volley
which falls inside the pepper-box itself. If the return must be
made on the defensive, hit the ball very low and gently, either
near the angle of the left-hand wall and the front wall, or
diagonally across the court to the right-hand angle. Under
no circumstances put up a ball high enough for the player
' in holes ' to smash down into the pepper-box or elsewhere.
If the return is on the offensive, leave the pepper-box, always
a dangerous position, for the middle of the court ; but if there
is the slightest possibility that the opponents may land the
ball in the pepper-box themselves, their stroke must be an-
ticipated, and the server (or the player ' in holes ', as the case
may be) must crouch under the front wall to retrieve the ball
from the pepper-box if necessary. The beginner always tends
to take up a permanent position actually in the pepper-box,
and by so doing not only spoils his partner's best shots, but
is likely to receive a ball in the eye or lip—most uncomfortable,
may I assure him.

On certain days even the best player will find himself

INCORRECT AND CORRECT.

Top : EVERYONE IS WRONG HERE. " D " IS NOT UNDERNEATH THE BALL, AND IS ALMOST CERTAIN TO MISS IT. " B " IS NOT LOOKING, WHILE " C " IS MANIFESTLY, AND REASONABLY, TERRIFIED. *Bottom :* THIS IS BETTER. " D " IS NOW WELL UNDERNEATH THE BALL, THOUGH HE DOES NOT LOOK AS IF HE INTENDS TO HIT IT VERY HARD. " C'S " POSITION IS GOOD, AS ALSO " B'S," THOUGH " B'S " EYE SHOULD BE ON THE BALL.

" A " WON'T GET IT UP IF IT COMES OUT FROM THE PEPPER-BOX AFTER — — — — —. (BALL OBSCURED BY GLOVE.) " B " WILL PROBABLY GET — — — — — UP, HOWEVER. " A " MIGHT GET ...., BUT IT IS UNLIKELY THAT HE COULD GET TO XXXXXXXXXX ; PERHAPS " B " COULD, THOUGH.

missing an unaccountable number of first cuts, and the fault
is usually to be found in his position. By moving a pace
forward, or a pace to the right or left, in all probability the
trouble will disappear. Finally, unless a player is very good
indeed with his left hand, the first cut which comes temptingly
to his left shoulder should be left severely alone. Even if
effective, it is at the best of times a difficult shot for the server,
yet it is always easy for his partner.

A word is necessary on the score of the duties of the server's
partner. Besides watching for all first cuts which hit the front
wall only, he must follow every first-cut which goes the normal
round, on the off-chance that the server, on purpose or by
mistake, will allow it to come out into the middle of the
court. Judicious calling of " Mine ", " Yours ", as the case
may be, will stop any confusion.

Before going on to consider the various tactics to be employed, a word must be said about the volley. It has often
been said that quite three strokes out of every four in a game
of Eton Fives are volleys. It would be more true to say that
three strokes out of every four made by a good player are
volleys. The offensive player uses the volley noticeably more
than the defensive player.

The volley is a vital factor where victory is concerned, for
it saves just that extra split second required to be ' one quicker
than the enemy '.

Volleys may be of two types : above the shoulder, always
hit overhand, and with a loose wrist ; and below the shoulder,
always hit underhand, generally with a stiff wrist and forearm.
The former is purely an offensive stroke. The latter is usually
defensive, except in the taking of the first cut, and will hardly
ever be used except on the top step. Its production is straight-
forward and requires no explanation ; most ' one-handed
players ' are able to use either hand for this stroke, even if
nowhere else in the game. During the course of the game
this stroke should not be used more frequently than necessary
(except in the case of the taking of first cuts) as only too often
it gives the other side the chance of a kill.

The overhand volley, or ' kill ', should emphatically be used
wherever possible. To time it accurately the eye must not
leave the ball for an instant until the stroke has actually been
played. The player should be slightly behind the ball at the
moment of striking. For a right-handed volley the feet should
be as in Fig. 3.

The *wrong* position is shown in Fig. 4.

The wrist must always be perfectly loose in order to ensure that the ball drops quickly on leaving the front wall. In nine cases out of ten a stiff wrist will cause the ball to go far out of court. It is of the greatest possible importance to be able to volley accurately with either hand, and is admittedly difficult to learn.

From the top step, the overhand volley may be usefully hit in many directions : (1) Into the pepper-box. This stroke

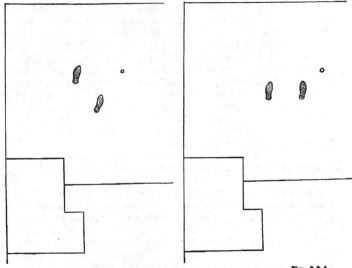

Figs. 3 & 4.

need not be played very hard and should aim either to fall in the Dead Man's Hole, or to hit the face of the pepper-box as near as possible to the floor. (2) So as to miss the pepper-box, and bounce near the left-hand step of the outer court. This stroke should often be used against players who are weak on their left hands, and will at times catch even left-handers unawares. (3) A gentle volley can sometimes be made to drop on top of an unsuspecting opponent who, crouching under the front wall, is waiting to retrieve a smash. To win a point in this way is most satisfactory. (4) The left-hander's

volley. This should be hit hard with a loose wrist from the
left-hand side of the upper court, and should bounce near the
right-hand back pillar. Delivered with all the weight of the
body behind it, the ball travels fast and is liable to hit the
projecting brickwork of the pillar in question.

From the lower court the volley over the back of the pepper-
box is most important (if a player is not tall enough, he should
never attempt this stroke, but should let the ball bounce. He
should then ' lift ' the ball over the pepper-box with only just
sufficient force behind it to enable it to go up. This gives his
opponents no chance to get in a kill). A tall player will
often volley a ball which comes over the top of the pepper-
box, and it is not difficult to make such shots drop so as to be
difficult to take, and on occasion they will enter the Dead
Man's Hole. A volley of this kind should never hit the left-
hand wall before hitting the front wall, and should preferably
hit the face of the pepper-box without touching the left-hand
wall at all.

From the back court, a volley which hits first the right-hand
wall, then the front wall, will often drop into the pepper-box
as in the first cut, but this stroke should not be played if one
of the opponents is in such a position that he can volley the
ball before it reaches the pepper-box ; for it is impossible to
impart the same cut as to a first cut, and therefore the opposing
side will be presented with an easy volley in an open court.
Care should be taken to see that the body is well underneath
the ball before making the stroke. Failure to observe this will
result in mistiming and consequently in misdirecting the ball.
Given a clear passage to the pepper-box, this stroke is most
useful, but it hardly ever occurs in good Fives, because the
pepper-box is never left unguarded. This is one of the few
strokes that may be played with a stiff wrist. K. C. Gandar
Dower, in particular, keeps his wrist stiff, and hits the ball
with the force of his whole arm, as if he were bowling the ball.

In general it may be said that a volley should hit the front
wall only, and the side walls as rarely as possible. It should
be remembered that the volley is the principal attacking
stroke in Eton Fives.

The majority of volleys are aimed to fall into the Dead Man's
Hole, from which it is almost impossible to retrieve the ball—
not quite impossible, for occasionally a hand will, by pure
accident or otherwise, contrive to ' lift ' the ball out, though
generally there is fierce argument as to whether the ball has

already bounced twice or not ; and one is bound to admit
that with reminiscence such shots increase in incredibility like
the length of the angler's tale, and the weight of his fish.
Beginner and expert alike, however, will find that a 12-inch
by 12-inch hole can be, and usually is exceedingly, almost
unnecessarily difficult to find. Therefore it is not to be
wondered that the rest of the pepper-box is a happy home
for ninety-nine out of every hundred shots originally intended
for the Dead Man's Hole. Since this is the case, it is most
important to learn to retrieve balls from the pepper-box.
Let it be said at once that very few balls which fall in the
pepper-box are untakeable, though the resulting stroke is
frequently most spectacular. (From the gallery the number
of balls which appear to fall 'dead' in the pepper-box is
most deceptive.) With practice the taking of balls from the
pepper-box becomes automatic, and it is very difficult to
defeat a good player on this score alone, unless he can first
be forced out of position. For this reason among good players
the rallies are of long duration, consisting as they do, of
constant volleying into, and retrieving out of, the pepper-box.
When the rally is ended, as often as not one player has been
completely unable to reach the ball : had he been in his proper
position of defence the stroke would have been easy for him.

    There are many accepted positions from which the retrieving
stroke may be played. The most usual, and the easiest for a
beginner, is to crouch under the front wall, facing the pepper-
box. The crouch must be adopted in order to avoid being
struck by an opponent's ball before it goes up. The player
should be well forward on his toes, ready to move in towards
the pepper-box should it be necessary. The objections to this
position are twofold : the player who is crouching in this
position is, of course, unable to volley, or to make any attacking
stroke ; and secondly, a cunning opponent will often drop a
gentle volley on to his back when he least expects it.

    It is advisable to use the left hand as much as possible in
the pepper-box—two hands, cupped together, should only be
used in emergency. The variety of strokes to be played from
this position is strictly limited, and two only are worth men-
tioning : the first should just clear the top of the pepper-box,
and should cling close to the left-hand wall. This stroke is
difficult to volley accurately, and is seldom killed, unless it
has been hit too high, or too far from the side wall. The
second stroke is played gently and does not rise high enough

to permit of an overhead volley, and will fall directly into the pepper-box again, and perhaps into the Dead Man's Hole. All other strokes from this position are liable to give the other side an easy kill.

Many players, possessed of a quick eye, prefer to take up a position by the side of the pepper-box, just below the step, and either volley the ball before it hits the pepper-box, or run forward and take it first bounce in the normal way. In general the first position may be said to be the easier, and should always be used if the opponents' stroke is coming from the lower step. Incidentally these remarks apply equally well to the taking of Blackguard Cut at Game Ball.

CHAPTER FIVE

E T O N   F I V E S (*continued*)

BY DAVID EGERTON

A FEW remarks on upper and lower court play will not be out of place. Eton Fives is, and should be, less than other games, a game which requires first and second strings. Yet that the game possesses many first-class first and second strings is undeniably true, as also is the sad inability of most first strings to play second fiddle, or for the second strings to take complete control of the attack. And both of these are pre-eminently necessary in Eton Fives, for the master of the upper court is master of the whole court. The player on the top step has 'first stab' at each stroke, and therefore should do his utmost to anticipate his opponents by planting a return on them before they are ready. The first duty of the player on the top step is to assume the initiative. This requires no little skill, great speed, an accurate eye, and a generous allowance of volleys with either hand. I have often seen games saved at the very last moment by one player deciding to 'take control'. Usually it means that no ball, or very few balls, will ever escape the eagle eye of the controller, and if he is quick enough and clever enough with his volleying he may tire or dishearten his opponents completely, by the sheer speed of his game. To do this effectively, great physical effort is required, and it cannot be sustained indefinitely. The importance of the volley on the top step cannot be over-stressed, as it is the essence of every victory. In a court where hazards and projections abound, delay is fatal : time is lost, and, hitting an unexpected ledge or angle, the ball will only too often disappear out of reach. On the top step, therefore, volley whenever possible.

The player on the top step has not only the task of making his own openings for a winning stroke, but he must also guard the pepper-box, and must take care not to give his opponents any possibility of making a winning stroke. He must also

know when and how to take a rest, and when to call upon his
partner to help him. He must remember that when on the
top step, he is for the time in charge of his side's destiny,
regardless of who is the master-mind of the combination.
But he should guard against trying to take too much for
himself ; a volley that will be difficult for him to take may be
quite easy for his partner. Co-operation is essential ; unless
two players can co-operate in partnership they will achieve
nothing. If there is any doubt as to who should take any
particular ball, the player on the top step should say " Yours "
or " Mine " as the case may be.

And now for the lower court. In elementary Fives, the
player on the lower step is kept well occupied with strokes
easy to reach, and, for him, hard to kill. If these strokes
occurred in first-class Fives, they would be killed dead every
time. They do not occur. But this does not mean that the
player in the lower court can at any period of the game be
lazy. From the beginning of each rally until the end, be he
partner of the server or of the player ' in holes ', he should
never be idle, even if during a rally of forty or fifty strokes he
may not touch the ball once. Quite apart from watching for
any balls which may come his way, he must also back up every
single stroke played by his partner on the top step. For on
the top step, playing at such close range, misjudgment is
bound to occur, and a player on the top step will often miss
the ball entirely or change his mind at the last moment, too
late to call. His partner in the back court must be waiting
for all these contingencies, and must be able to continue his
partner's plan of attack, without leaving any part of the court
unguarded. During the rally the player in the lower court
may be called upon to make all manner of curious strokes,
from the volley over the top of the pepper-box, to the half-
volley, most difficult and unsatisfactory of strokes, from the
back step.

Provided the player on the lower step is paying due attention, it is difficult to defeat him outright, for most of the
strokes are easy to return up from the open part of the court.
He must, however, guard against the four favourite attacking
strokes which can come from the opponents : (1) That which
comes low over the pepper-box, grazing the left-hand wall
during its career. This ball just hits, or just misses, the ledge
before bouncing, and in either case is difficult to return.
(2) That which, hit from the right-hand side of the upper

court, just misses the pepper-box, and bounces near the left-hand back pillar of the court, sometimes hitting the projecting brickwork to make matters more difficult. (3) While on the look out for (2) care must be taken to see that the ball does not hit the right-hand *side* of the pepper-box, and fall into the middle of the court to the player's wrong foot. (4) He must beware of the Left-Hander's Volley (see above). If a player is defending the back of the pepper-box, the left-hander's volley will often take him completely unawares.

In general young players are far too apt to concentrate on the pepper-box, and on the pepper-box alone. Quite recently I was watching a match in which two right-handed players nearly lost to two weaker left-handed players, simply because the right-handers insisted on plastering the left hands of the left-handers, leaving the right-hand part of the court completely empty, except for the few occasions when the *left-handers* used the left-handers' volley to good advantage. The majority of young players do not use their heads half enough. They like to hit every ball as hard as possible, no matter where or when. Now it must be admitted that it is often possible to demoralize opponents by hard hitting—tempered by good judgment. For hard hitting carries with it a host of disadvantages : the likelihood of bruised hands, the danger of hitting the ball on to a ledge or out of court, and finally the number of times the ball hit hard into, say, the pepper-box will come out again, only to give the opponents an easy kill, whereas a gentle stroke would have fallen dead. Therefore watch for your opponents' weaknesses of hand or stroke, and then plaster any defects you can find in their armour. Never hit harder than you need. Try and get both opponents on the run. A hard and deep volley followed by a gentle one pitching at the foot of the top step will often make both players run, and an alternate short and long game of this kind will often effectively tire and dishearten your opponents.

Try and avoid changing your mind. Hesitation will prove your undoing, and inaccurate first thoughts will do less damage than tardy second thoughts.

Never play a ' tiddly ' game, unless you are firmly convinced of your ability to beat your opponent at it. ' Tiddly ' is perhaps a slang word to use, but it is the only word which adequately describes the untidy messing (more slang) from corner to corner, entailed in such tactics. The endless repetition of ' pushes ' just above the line more often than not ends in a let. If, however, you happen to have the art (it is given to few) of looking one way the while you gently lift the ball just above the ledge in the opposite direction, so much the better—but it requires both practice and patience, together with luck, and perhaps some measure of deceit!

Never muddle your partner. If you keep on changing your mind, or start taking balls which are not strictly speaking yours, you will upset him, a thing which would not be over-looked by skilful opponents. He presumably makes up his mind what to do if you miss the ball, and if necessary or possible will act accordingly. Therefore do all you can to help him.

During the rally avoid hitting into the middle of the court, and note that the ball should usually hit the side walls after, and almost never before, the first bound.

Remember above all things that the essence of the game is speed, i.e. making your stroke before your opponents have time to prepare for it. But do not be so eager to prepare for your next stroke that you impede them in their attempts to make their shots. Half the art of Fives consists in getting out of your opponents' way. And, as we have seen in the Service, and the Blackguard Cut at Game Ball, Eton Fives is essentially a game of courtesies. A player who does not do his utmost to avoid getting in the way is a serious nuisance. Occasions will arrive—and often—when it will be impossible for you to move quickly enough to allow your opponents to play their stroke as they wish, and in every case a let should be offered before they have time to ask for it. It will be seen that Laws 8, 9, and 10 deal with the different aspects of the let, with a note at the end of Law 9 to the effect that " if there is no Umpire, a let is generally allowed ". Now I think I am voicing the feelings of most Fives players if I say that the great feature of the game is the lack of any provision for any form of umpire or marker. We are right in insisting that the innate courtesy of the game is such that in nearly every case no umpire is required or even welcome—a most satisfactory state of affairs which will be envied by many other games. None the less in the heat of the moment certain players are apt to show argumentative tendencies, and in these cases an umpire should immediately be appointed.

Temperament and temper will often be the deciding factor in an otherwise even match. A player, however good, loses efficiency and accuracy when rattled, and many a game has

been retrieved out of the fire by a cool and determined last-
minute effort. The difficulty is that only experience will tell
a player just when is the psychological moment to start his
' effort '.

Little has been said in this chapter on the theory of stroke
production, or indeed on the numerous strokes that are made
in the normal course of the rally. It is my belief that these
strokes will come naturally, provided that sufficient care is
taken to keep the eye on the ball, and to place the feet correctly. I do not therefore intend to describe all these strokes,
since space would not permit. One stroke in particular must,
however, be mentioned, for in the future of Fives it may play
an important part.

It will be remembered that Pelota was mentioned as being
one of the forefathers of Fives, and the stroke here described
comes from Spain and Pelota. It was evolved by a Spaniard,
C. A. Aguirre, when at Highgate School. Partnered by A. H.
Fabian, Aguirre used it most effectively when they won the
Kinnaird Cup together. Unfortunately, Aguirre has now
returned to his native Spain, and since his departure the stroke
has not been developed. Aguirre more or less perfected the
stroke for his own use, but whether because the rest of us
have not had the peculiar advantage of a pelota education,
or because he had not time, he has not imparted his skill
even to other Highgate players to such a high degree as to
make the stroke a true and useful part of a Fives player's
repertoire. The Highgate players of to-day do use it, but
without that spontaneity and effectiveness which are necessary to disguise the stroke and deceive the opponent.

Let me quote from *The Times*, in which F. B. Wilson wrote
as follows :

" Aguirre is a left-handed player, neat but severe, with all
the left-hander's natural advantages in a game specially made
for the left-hander. He has, moreover, the honour to introduce
a new stroke to this venerable game. In taking a ball that
has dropped to knee-high or lower, the ordinary play has
been a purely defensive stroke, the main object of which, and
one not by any means always attained, has been to avoid
allowing one of the opposition to make an easy volley for
himself. Aguirre attacks with his left hand, with a stroke
peculiar so far to himself. His stroke is a straight stab, very
like a short jab to the heart, with the hand palm upwards,
slanting very slightly towards the ground, and the back of

TACTICS.

Top : " D " HAS MADE A POOR LEFTHANDER'S VOLLEY, BUT " A " CANNOT QUITE GET TO IT. NOTICE " B " WHO HAS EXPECTED IT TO BE AIMED FOR THE PEPPER-BOX.

Centre : " C " WILL GET THIS UP. NOTICE THE LEFT-HAND RIGHT BACK, AND THE BODY NOT TOO CLOSE TO THE WALL. IF " B," WOULD KINDLY LOOK THIS WAY TOWARDS THE BALL HE MIGHT BE ABLE TO KILL IT, OTHERWISE HE WILL PROBABLY GET HIT IN THE FACE.

Bottom : " B " JUMPING TO SAVE FIRST CUT GOING OUT, OTHERWISE A " GOOD 'UN." " D " IS TRYING TO STOP HIM GETTING TO IT.

the wrist and forearm parallel to the ground. The hand is shot forward very quickly, and for a distance of about eighteen inches. The stab under and along the ball imparts exactly the same cut as does the racket with a very open face to a racket ball. The opponent who tries to volley Aguirre's stab stroke·usually misses it, the first and second times, by inches : later he hits the ball on the under side of the hand, and if he tries an ordinary kill, he hits the ball down. This stroke is mentioned because it is obviously of the greatest importance as turning a defence into an attack. Aguirre can make a really hard stroke in this peculiar way of his, and brings the ball down into Dead Man's Hole."

I have never had the opportunity of seeing Aguirre play, but I have seen many other players attempt the same stroke, though none of them has been able to make a really hard stroke, such as Aguirre could. None of them, I am assured, has been able to play it nearly so effectively as Aguirre, though it has on occasion proved useful. Perhaps someone else will perfect its use, and impart the skill to other players.

And finally the question of training, match-play, and staleness. As at cricket, so in Eton Fives, staleness is wellnigh impossible owing to the variety of the game, and the long-winded course of that greatest of all teachers—experience. But everyone who plays regularly knows the dreadful feeling of not being able to do justice to oneself during the course of a game. It usually starts after a rag game, or when one is overtired, and it may last for weeks at a time. I know of no satisfactory cure save perhaps to try and get a game with three players who are all better than oneself ; on these occasions one is apt to play better than usual automatically. In any case the ' Don't-Care-Two-Hoots ' method of playing oneself back to form by sheer hard hitting, so often indulged in, should not be adopted—it never succeeds in its object.

Nobody trains for Eton Fives, for Eton Fives is a mere by-product of our national craze for sport, and most good players are already in good training for their other sporting interests. In few games, however, can soundness in wind and limb be more important. The speed at which the game is played and the short distance and time between the ball striking the wall and striking the glove make rapid accommodation and co-ordination essential. Regular sleep and a temperate life are as important for taking first cuts as for mastering difficult bowling.

When playing matches never slack off until the last point
has actually been won. Extraordinary things happen at
Eton Fives (though no more so than at other games), and
three or four slack points may be just sufficient to allow the
losers to find an altogether new form, while the winners may
equally miraculously strike an unaccountably long bad patch.

Always try and assume the offensive, find out your opponents'
weaknesses, and plaster them. If one kind of game does not
succeed, try another. Never under any circumstances play
your opponents' game unless you are better at it than they.

If you start badly and fail to bring off spectacular strokes,
do not get annoyed. Anger only helps your opponents.
Above all, never get angry with your partner. He is doing
his best, and both must work together. A divided partnership
is as good as a third player on the opponents' side.

And lastly, however bleak the situation, never give up
hope.

The following Hints on Eton Fives were written by the
late G. Townsend Warner, assuredly one of the greatest players
who have ever lived. "As a coach he was wonderful, as
anyone reading his Essay on Fives will understand : for
practically all there is to know of Eton Fives is contained, in
essence at least, in his short hints. His observations on ' Lets '
show, as no words can show, his passionate insistence on the
spirit of the game." Certainly no book on Eton Fives would
be complete without the inclusion of these Hints. I am very
grateful to Miss S. Townsend Warner for giving me permission
to have them printed here.

"Fives is popularly supposed to be played with the *hands*.
This is only part of the truth. It is also played with the
LEGS and the HEAD. Few things are hard if you are in the
right place ; nothing is easy if you are in the wrong place.
Therefore :

" 1. NEVER LOSE SIGHT OF THE BALL. Players in the top
court should keep their heads out of the way, but should
always keep their eyes on the ball when it is in the back court.
If you are on the look-out and your opponent makes a weak
stroke you can see it in time to kill it ; therefore always
watch the ball all the time.

" 2. VOLLEY THE EASY ONES. Volleys can only be reached
by moving for them. Be ready to move for them. The
underhand volley (ball well below the shoulder) is rarely a
good stroke. It should only be used in defence.

" 3. PLAY WITH YOUR HEAD. Don't be content to hit the buttress ; try for the hole ; place the ball well out of your opponent's reach. Direction is more important even than pace. It is not necessary to knock the stuffing out of the ball every shot.

" 4. Avoid as far as possible either taking or causing ' lets '. You must get well out of your opponent's way at once. He is entitled, not only to get the ball up, but to have the best possible chance of hitting it. Should he, however, grasp you with one hand while he hits it with the other, you may remonstrate with him.

" TO THE PLAYER HITTING THE FIRST CUT.

" 1. Never take a Serve you don't like : not even from your tutor.

" 2. Take pains with the first cut ; it is the best chance you will have of getting the other side out. Hit hard and low : if possible, get ' cut ' on the ball.

" 3. If your enemy keeps on getting up one kind, try another :

" (a) More round : i.e. more of the right-hand wall, and as hard as you can.

" (b) Slower and with a great deal of ' cut '.

" 4. Jump up into the top court immediately you have hit the first cut. Don't wait to see if your opponent gets it up ; you will be too late then. Jump up at once beside him, and you will often be in time to get an easy volley and kill him ' with the second barrel '. If he knows you are there ready to destroy him, you will often frighten him into missing or making a bad stroke.

" TO THE PLAYER TAKING THE FIRST CUT.

" 1. Get it up : anything is better than missing it.

" 2. The easiest way of getting very hard-hit first cuts is to hit hard at them with the right hand. If you only hit quick enough they are easy. If you let them get too close to you · or to your left hand they are difficult.

" 3. Remember that anything that comes to your left hand will go round to your partner if you get out of the way, so leave these. Let them pass either behind you or in front of you.

" 4. If you are constantly being beaten by the first cut, change your position and stand either (a) more to your own left, i.e. farther up the left-hand wall, or (b) farther forward, that is out of your corner towards the corner from which the ball is coming. Or (*c*) step in to meet them, or (*d*) stoop more.

" 5. First cuts can often be returned by hitting them against the left-hand wall first.

" 6. Not a bad stroke is to send them back high over the box, near the left-hand wall.

" To the Top Court generally.

" 1. Keep close to your opponent when playing gently (sniggling) in the top court.

" 2. The best place is on his inner side, i.e. on his right when you are near the left-hand wall ; and on his left when you are near the right-hand wall—you will not then have to run round him, and volleys will come easier.

" 3. Don't sniggle except in defence. As soon as you get a chance put the ball back over the box, close to the left-hand wall, and far back.

" 4. If you and your partner have put up an easy volley to the other side, don't despair ; don't say ' Oh ! ' ; run up under the line near the left-hand wall. The ball is almost certain to come there. Never put your head down so that you cannot see the ball.

" 5. Never stand in the Box. By doing so
(1) You spoil your partner's best strokes ;
(2) You are a victim to an opponent's volley.

" 6. Hit the ball ; don't hold it.

" 7. In case of a doubtful one, call ' Mine ' or ' Yours ' at once.

" 8. If your opponent is in difficulties far back in the left-hand side of the court, come well back from the front wall on the chance of a volley. It is generally a mistake to stand close to the front wall, except in defence. You cannot make a good stroke if you are too close.

" 9. Practise volleying with your left hand, you get more chances with it ; and especially practise the left-hand volley which keeps the ball on the left-hand side of the court. A left-hand volley across the court, i.e. to the right side, is generally useless, unless you can hit it very hard.

" 10. Never use two hands when one will do.

" To the Back Court.

" 1. Look out for volleys. They are easy to you and deadly to the other side.

" 2. Goliath can always volley the strokes that come back over the box ; very often with the right hand by getting close enough against the wall : but the left hand is best if possible. David must let these pitch.

" 3. Hit hard and low. Play for the buttress and for the hole, or for the pillar at the back of the left wall.

" 4. If you get a difficult one, don't try and make a stroke from it. Play it back high on the left or somewhere out of reach.

" 5. An easy one can often be hit with excellent effect round the right-hand wall, like a first cut, but remember :

(a) Hit it pretty hard.

(b) The ball will drop a great deal, so don't aim too low.

(c) The stroke is not good if your opponent on the top court is on the left-hand side of the court—if he is crouching on the right-hand side of the court, it is very good.

" 6. Never call 'Mine' to your top court partner if he has the chance of a volley. Call at once if you see that it will be difficult for him.

" 7. Be ready to back up your partner in the top court in case of a return coming round. Even if you didn't expect it to come, you ought to have. A really good player in the back court is always ready to take anything his partner misses ; but there are not many players quite so good as this."

D

RULES OF RUGBY FIVES

CHAPTER SIX

RULES OF RUGBY FIVES

(As approved by the Rugby Fives Association)

DEFINITIONS

The game is played in a court enclosed by four walls. The ' front ' wall is distinguished by a board of wood running across it at an even height from the ground.

The wall opposite the front wall is the ' back ' wall, and the two adjoining walls, as the players stand facing the front wall, are respectively the ' right ' side wall and the ' left 'side wall.

The game may be played between two or four players, i.e. as Singles, or Doubles.

The throwing up of the ball into play is known as the ' service ', and the player who hits the ball thus thrown is known as the ' striker ' (who is said to be ' out ' or ' down '), his opponent being known as the ' server ' (who is said to be ' in ' or ' up ').

RULES OF THE SINGLES GAME

1. At the commencement of a game a preliminary rally shall be played. The winner of this becomes the server, and the loser, striker.

2. SERVICE. The server must ' serve ' the ball by throwing it up so that it strikes the front wall first, above the board, and then one of the side walls, in such a manner as the striker may require. If the striker so desire, he may throw the ball up for himself.

3. The striker may not return a service that does not conform to Rule 2.

4. RETURN OF SERVICE. The striker must return the ball, after the first bounce and before the second, so that the ball strikes first the side wall against which the service has been thrown and then the front wall.

5. After the service and its return the opponents shall alternately hit the ball, before the second bounce, on to the front wall above the board, either directly or after it has hit the side and/or back walls. No second attempt to hit a ball may be made after it has once been touched.

6. BLACKGUARD. Should the return of service hit the front wall, either first or after previously hitting the opposite side wall (such a return being known as a ' blackguard '), the server may take it as if it had been correctly returned, provided he calls out ' Taken ' before hitting the ball. Such decision having been once given cannot be revoked.

The striker may not intentionally stop a blackguard. (See Rule 8b.)

When the server requires one point to win the game he may not take a blackguard.

7. SCORING. The player who first scores 15 points (except as provided when the score reaches game-ball-all) wins the game.

Only the server can score points. When the server wins a rally, he scores one point. When the striker wins a rally, he becomes server.

Should each player score 14 points, the first player to score 2 points wins the game.

8. A rally is won by a player if—

(a) his opponent fails to hit the ball (except as provided under 9d), or hits it after the second bounce, or hits it on to or below the board, or against the roof, or otherwise out of the confines of the court, or on to the floor before hitting the front wall.

Note (1). When the server requires one point to win the game, the striker is not penalized if he returns the service not more than twice consecutively on to or below the board, or against the roof, or otherwise outside the confines of the court.

Note (2). Should a player strike his opponent with a ball which would not have gone ' up ' (i.e. been correctly returned to the front wall), he nevertheless loses the rally.

(b) his opponent, being striker, returns more than two consecutive untaken blackguards, or intentionally stops a blackguard.

(c) he causes the ball, after it has hit the front wall, to strike his opponent before it has bounced, other than in the case provided for under 9c.

(d) if his opponent causes the ball, after it has hit the front wall, to strike himself before it has bounced. This also applies to blackguards.

(e) his opponent hits the ball otherwise than with the hand or forearm.

9. LETS. A let is allowed, and the rally shall not count if—

(a) a player strikes his opponent with a ball which would have gone ' up '.

(b) a player causes the ball, after it has hit the front wall, to strike himself after it has bounced.

(c) a player is prevented by his opponent from correctly returning the ball. Should a player, though impeded, hit the ball so that it go ' up ', he may claim a let at once : otherwise the rally shall continue.

(d) the striker, when about to return the service, fails to hit the ball, or changes his mind and calls out ' No ' before hitting the ball, even if it accidentally go ' up '.

10. The umpire's decision is final.

RULES OF THE DOUBLES GAME

The Rules of the Singles Game shall apply to the Doubles Game, and wherever the words ' server ', ' striker ', ' opponent ', or ' player ' are used in the Rules of the Singles Game, such words shall, wherever possible, be taken to include his partner in the Doubles Game.

1. All four players shall take part in the preliminary rally.

2. The server and his partner are known as ' hands '. The side winning the preliminary rally shall have only one hand.

3. The server remains ' in ' until his side loses a rally, whereupon his partner shall serve (except as provided for in Rule 2). When his side loses another rally, his opponents become servers.

4. The side that is ' down ' must change strikers after every point scored by their opponents.

5. If the wrong player serves or strikes, the mistake must be pointed out before the end of the rally, otherwise the rally counts ; but at the next ' hand ', the pairs shall revert to their correct order.

6. Only the server may take the return of service, but either he or his partner may elect to take a blackguard.

CHAPTER SEVEN

RUGBY FIVES

BY JOHN ARMITAGE

"FIVES," writes the Rev. J. G. Wood in his book, *The Boys' Modern Playmate,* and he is speaking particularly of Rugby Fives, "is a capital game for a back yard." This is no sentence of derision but a compliment paid by a man who realizes a true value of the game ; a tribute to a sport that glories in its simplicity. For Rugby Fives is above everything a simple game, that through its adaptability has appealed to its many followers. One wall, three walls, four walls, that is the history of the development of the court in which the game is played ; the bare hand, a hand bound with skins and cords, a gloved hand ; any ball, a standard ball : that is the history of the gear necessary for playing the game.

It is true that now, and at last, efforts have been made to standardize the courts, determining their proper measurements, the height of the board, and to issue an authorized version of the rules, and more about this will be found in its proper place. But regulations add little to the beauty of a game, only they make it more convenient for match play. For, of course, when court conditions are so varied as they are at present, the home side can claim a very big advantage indeed.

Simplicity alone, however, is not enough to give a game a wide appeal, and the use of this word ' simplicity ' must not be misunderstood. Fives is not an easy game to play well, but it is an easy game to play. That is, a game does not demand elaborate preparations ; it needs no expensive gear, while the time necessary for playing a game, except in matches, is extremely short. Given a partner of equal standard to yourself, half an hour is sufficient for anyone who is only seeking exercise, and it is as an exercise that Fives is deservedly so popular. There is, perhaps, no game equal to Rugby Fives for bringing into play so many muscles of the body in so short a time. In the first place, to be a player of any standing at all, one should be able to play reasonably well with either hand ;

55

placing accurately with both left and right is essential to success, while although one will be naturally stronger with one than the other, the one-handed player is deservedly useless. Without a racket one must get to the ball every time oneself. This is no easy matter and means running, bending, twisting and turning, which denotes real exercise and not mere fatigue from a great deal of rushing about.

I said just now that Rugby Fives was not an easy game to play well. It is not, for it demands the greatest concentration and accuracy on all those points that go towards making a man a good games player. Suppleness and balance of body, a good eye, neat and quick footwork are all as necessary to Fives players as to exponents of other games, perhaps more so, for the whole area of play is so confined, that to see quickly and move with precision is of supreme importance. Nevertheless, much of the charm of this game lies in the fact that as long as two or four players of more or less the same standard are playing together, they can get almost as much fun and exercise out of their game as can any four players, however good they may be.

Fives is very definitely fun. It is a sociable game, in which universal reputations cannot be lost or won. A Fives court is rarely remarkable for the tenseness of the silence, broken only by the clock of balls against the walls and the thud of a man's hand ; it is rather a jolly place, because it is so extremely intimate. There is time in between the rallies to admire the play of an opponent and there is never reason to doubt that the next good shot may be one of your own. Perhaps this applies more to doubles than to singles, for singles can be very exhausting and not in the least jolly. But all the same, the grim professional spirit is entirely absent, although this we shall find was not always the case, as in the days of Jack Cavanagh, a man who was accustomed to playing for a wager or his dinner.

In any case a more auspicious time than the present could not have been found in the whole history of the game for writing about Fives. Even those who like myself are enthusiasts, and believe it to be a national pastime, are satisfied that what has been done in the last few years is as important for its welfare as anything that has occurred in the whole history of its six centuries of history. Fives is a game to be played in order to be understood and loved, for its fascination, so slender in appearance, is deep and glorious for all those who look for enjoyment and not for honour from their games. Few people, who have played it once, have failed to regret the day when they could play no more.

HOW THE GAME IS PLAYED

At the present time it is almost impossible to find two sets of Fives courts which are identical to one another in every respect. The differences may be slight, an inch or two either way, the surface composition or the colour of the walls, but they are always there and it would be impossible to make an accurate statement of their dissimilarities, without resorting to a catalogue of the particulars of every court. I have no intention of attempting such a task. In another place I shall have ample opportunity to describe these differences in a generalized form with especial reference to the alterations they may make to the course of a game. Here it is my intention to describe a Rugby Fives court, just as it has been recommended by the Rugby Fives Association as recently as 1931, and to imagine, then, a game as it would be played in that court.

A Rugby Fives court should be 28 feet long and 18 feet wide, bounded on all four sides by walls. The front or ' facing ' wall is 15 feet in height and is distinguished from the other three walls by a board of wood, the sounding board, which runs in a horizontal position across it at an even height of 2 feet 6 inches from the floor of the court. Opposite to the front wall is the ' back ' wall, 6 feet in height, " and the two adjoining walls, as the players stand facing the front wall, are respectively the ' right ' side wall and the ' left ' side wall ". Measuring from the front wall, the height of the side walls is 15 feet for the first 12 feet, thence sloping down to 6 feet to meet the back.

The colour of the floor is red ; the colour of the walls is black. The door should be in the centre of the back wall, having the same surface and the same resistance as the walls, and the handle should be flush with the surface. Usually a spectators' gallery is to be found situated above the back wall.

If you will turn to the illustrations a moment, you will see that in one or two particulars the courts in which the photographs are taken do not coincide with the above description. The height of the side walls is uniform all the way, about 15 feet, instead of sloping down to 6 feet towards the back, while the whole of the back wall, instead of having a horizontal line drawn across it at a height of 6 feet from the ground and all above it being considered ' out of play ', is accounted to be ' in play '.

A Fives ball is hard, weighing 1⅛ oz. or 1¼ oz. It has an inner core of cork, which is bound with felt strips, which is again bound with thread, and the whole is encased in a covering of white leather and sewn. The gloves used to protect the hands of the players are many and according to the personal likes and dislikes of the individual using them, but the novice is advised to pad his hands well, for bruised hands recover very slowly unless they are completely rested.

It is best, at first, to wear two pairs of gloves, an inner pair and an outer pair. The inner pair should be of wash leather with padded strips along the palm side of the knuckles and along the fingers. The outer pair should be of good, pliable leather, of a sort that is sold especially for the purpose by sports outfitting shops. It is always worth while buying a good pair, as they adapt themselves easily to the hand and last an average good player four or five seasons. The importance of this subject of gloves can be realized by all players who have neglected to bring their own to a match and in consequence have been obliged to borrow a pair. Gloves are not a mere shield to the hand, they are a personal possession without which a player is a different man. They are never too old as long as they still hang together, for a new pair invariably puts the balance of the hand right out, as the thickness of the padding and the stiffness of the leather denies the touch. Many people, especially beginners, make the mistake of wearing an inner pair of gloves of wool ; these can be a greater handicap than the player realizes, for they will deaden the speed of a shot and give no resistance to the short sharp stroke. Playing with bare hands, as is encouraged at some schools, although ideal as far as balance is concerned, is a foolhardy practice. Such players can rarely stand up to hard hitting, while a few carefully controlled shots down the side walls will soon break their nails and their spirits. I cannot recall any good player who does not use gloves, except as an occasional show of bravado.

The best arrangement, if your hands are horny enough to stand it, is to wear only the pair of inner wash leather gloves with the padded strips. These give plenty of resistance without destroying the touch, and being light the balance of the hand is not destroyed. One well-known player is uniquely successful with an ordinary pair of kid leather gloves, but the sound of the contact is so distressing, that it is a practice I would prefer to discourage.

It takes many seasons of play for a man to become immune

from bruises and some people could never achieve this ideal. Accordingly, and as in many other things, the best cure for bruises is in prevention. Bad bruises, that is when the bone is injured beneath the skin, are not only very painful but permanent. There is no cure. If you must play, it is probably still the wisest course to use raw meat inside the glove against the wound, but raw meat is heavy as well as disgusting, and I shall always prefer to use a wad of cotton-wool.

About the equipment for a game there is nothing left to say. A pair of rubber-soled shoes is all that is essential together with the gloves. Most Rugby Fives players, however, prefer to play in shorts and a zephyr, for the long white trouser which tradition demands an Eton Fives player should wear can be both hot and cumbersome.

CHAPTER EIGHT

R U G B Y   F I V E S (*continued*)

BY JOHN ARMITAGE

THE SINGLES GAME

I SHALL content myself here by giving a short description of how a singles game of Rugby Fives is played, embodying into the context as many of the actual rules as I find possible and convenient. Later I shall describe in what manner the game of doubles differs from that of singles, and finally I shall write of the art of playing the game with reference to both forms. As far as possible when referring to a rule of the game I shall use the actual definition of the Rugby Fives Association, as it is important that there should be no difference between what I write and what is written in the book of approved rules.

A word or two first about the technical use of words, which may be found in the following pages. The player who throws the ball up into play, in a manner to be described, is called the ' server ', and the player who strikes the ball thus served to him is called the ' striker '. The server may be spoken of as ' up ' or ' hand in ', and the striker as ' down ' or ' hand out '.

Before a match can start it is necessary to hold a preliminary rally to determine who is to be server or ' up ', and who is to be striker or ' down '. The winner of this rally becomes server and the loser, striker. The match then begins by the server throwing the ball up in such a way that it hits first the front wall above the board, and then one of the side walls, before bouncing on the ground. It is for the striker to decide which corner best suits his requirements. In all probability if he is right-handed he will choose the right-hand corner, while if he is left-handed, he will choose the other. He may have the ball served up exactly as he wishes ; that is, as softly as he likes, or as hard, as high or as low. The striker is not required to accept the throw of the service unless it pleases him, and he

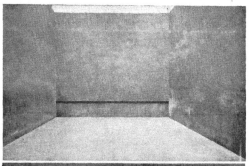

Plates **XV, XVI & XVII**

Top : THE COURT.
THE GAME IS PLAYED IN A COURT ENCLOSED BY FOUR WALLS

Centre : SERVICE.
" 2 " IS ABOUT TO THROW THE BALL UP IN THE RIGHT-HAND CORNER AND HE
IS STANDING BEHIND AND A LITTLE TO THE RIGHT OF " 1."

Bottom : BALANCE.
AS HE STRUCK THE BALL HE THREW THE BALANCE OF HIS BODY ON TO THE
LEFT FOOT.

may, if he should so desire, serve the ball for himself. However, it is not, as a rule, considered very satisfactory for the
striker to serve the ball for himself; it is confusing for all concerned in the game, and annoying; it is usually only resorted
to when the server is continuously unable, through accident or
nature, to serve as he is desired. The striker is not allowed to
return a service which does not conform to the above ruling.

When returning the service the striker must hit the ball after
the first bounce and before the second, so that the ball strikes
first the side wall, against which the service has been thrown,
and then the front wall. That is to say, if the striker has asked
for the ball to be served in the right-hand corner, he cannot
return it by striking it in the left-hand corner. The rally then
proceeds with alternate strokes from each of the two players
hitting the ball either at the volley or before the second bounce
" on to the front wall above the board, either directly or after
it has hit the side and/or back walls ". A player is not allowed
to make a second attempt at hitting the ball up, if he has
already touched the ball once. When playing his shot, the
player can, of course, make use of the side walls to gain his
angle, but the ball must strike the front wall every time above
the board either directly from the hand, or off one of the side
walls.

If the striker, when he is returning a service which has been
thrown up in the right-hand corner, hits the front wall first
instead of the right-hand side wall, or hits the left-hand side
and then the front wall, his stroke is known as a ' blackguard '
and it may be returned by the server, as if it had been played
correctly, providing the server call out " Taken " before he
plays his shot. Similarly, a service thrown up in the left-hand
corner and returned direct by the striker to the front wall or
hitting the right-hand side wall and then the front wall is
called a ' blackguard ' and may be taken by the server. Once
the server has called out " Taken ", he cannot alter his decision.
On the other hand the striker who has been guilty of a blackguard cannot intentionally stop it or prevent the server from
taking it should he wish to do so. He will, however, frequently
stop it unintentionally, for blackguards will usually occur from
over-hitting straight on to the front wall, rebounding too
quickly for the striker to escape. If the ball rebounds so quickly
that it hits the striker before it bounces, the striker loses the
point, but after the bounce it counts a let and the point is
replayed. If he should strike more than two consecutive black-

guards, which are not taken by the server, the striker loses the point, but this does not apply to 'match point'. At 'match point' the striker cannot lose the game by playing more than two blackguards, nor can the server call "Taken" and return a blackguard.

There is another concession to the striker at 'match point'; he is not penalized should he return the service at this point of the game on to the board or below it, providing he does not do it more than twice consecutively. Nor is he penalized should he return the service elsewhere outside the confines of the court at 'match point', again providing that he does not do it more than twice consecutively.

It is necessary, at this point, to state concisely how a point may be won. A player wins the rally if his opponent fails to return the ball in accordance with the ruling given above. That is, he wins the point if his opponent fails to hit the ball, hits the ball after the second bounce, or hits the ball on to the ground—or anywhere else that may be deemed out of court—before hitting the front wall. He will also win the rally should his opponent return the ball with any part of his body other than his hand and forearm.

The scoring in singles play is not difficult, although for matches and doubles it is often desirable to have an umpire. The player who first obtains fifteen points has won the game, unless the score at one time is 14—14 or game-ball-all, when the player who first scores the next two points has won the match. No point can be scored by a player who is not 'up' or server. When the server wins a rally he has gained a point, but when the striker wins a rally, he becomes server. Thus, if the score were 5—3, and the striker wins the rally, the score is reversed but not changed, and becomes 3—5.

There is one difficulty that all court games, where both teams defend the same ground, have in common, their system of awarding 'lets'. A let nullifies the result of a rally and is awarded because in the opinion of the umpire the point has been unfairly gained. Unfortunately the umpire at Rugby Fives is quite unable to decide from his position in the gallery whether a let is justifiable or not, and in consequence when a player claims a let, it is customary for him to receive one. Players, too, have got into the habit of offering lets to their opponents and rather than be thought mean, they are over-generous, which often results in the practice being reduced to an absurdity. It should be the maxim of all Fives players that

' too many lets spoil the game ', for however well meant the inquiry " Have a let ? " may be, it is often for the self-respecting player who has missed his shot, additional ignominy. In bad doubles play lets are of frequent occurrence, but there is really no excuse for the practised player who is constantly claiming them.

The difficulty arises over the rule that says that a player may claim a let and the rally shall not count if " a player is prevented by his opponent from correctly returning the ball. Should a player, though impeded, hit the ball so that it go ' up ', he may claim a let at once ; otherwise the rally shall continue." This rule can easily be abused, and yet it is impossible to make it more definite. The same difficulty is experienced in Squash Rackets ; for if the ruling did not stand it might encourage many objectionable practices. But it leaves much to be desired.

In the first place the obvious aim of one's opponent is to prevent you from correctly returning the ball, and as he cannot expect to do this by speed and ' winners ' alone, he must resort to guile, trying to deceive you with the pace and direction of the ball. He will attempt what is called, ' masking the return ', and if he is clever at it, he will catch you on the wrong foot and running up on the wrong side of him. You are unsighted and you bump into him. That is your fault and you should claim no let, but there are more difficult cases, when it is partly your fault and when you might have retrieved the ball had he not moved into you believing that you were coming up on the other side, as you should have been. The question to be quickly decided is whether you were unsighted by the clumsiness of your opponent or his failure to get out of your line of vision quickly enough, or by his greater skill in manœuvring you out of position. It is not an easy question and it is best never to accept a let unless, knowing where the ball is, you are actually prevented by your opponent's physical bulk from reaching it.

There is little difficulty over the other lets that are allowed. If a player strikes his opponent with the ball which would have gone up, if unimpeded, a let is awarded. Again if a player strikes the ball against the front wall, causing it to rebound on to him after it has bounced, he is allowed a let, as also when the striker about to return the service changes his mind before hitting the ball and cries out " No ", even if the ball should accidentally go up.

CHAPTER NINE

RUGBY FIVES (*continued*)

BY JOHN ARMITAGE

THE DOUBLES GAME

AS might be expected, the Doubles game of Rugby Fives is more complicated than that of Singles, but the difficulties are more apparent than real. Since both doubles and singles are played in the same-size court, the former is less strenuous, and most people, at any rate after they have left school, prefer it. But apart from the fact that singles can be unduly strenuous, a really good game of doubles is the better fun of the two, although more difficult to obtain. This is not strange, for a good double requires three other players of equal skill to yourself, while a single, besides needing only one other person, can allow a considerable margin of difference between the adroitness of the two players and yet be enjoyed. In a single a player may practise shots even against a weaker opponent, but in a double he has not only to adapt himself to the two standards of the opposition, plying the weaker when it would be more fun to attack the other, but he has to recognize obligations to his partner as well. To begin with he must play to win. Then, if he is a better player than his partner, it will be hard for him to curb his desire to take more than his fair share of the game, while, if he is worse, he is often called upon to efface himself, when his natural inclination is to do quite differently. But these are troubles which belong to all doubles games and to nearly all team games ; the dilemma between doing what is best for one's side and selfish amusement.

However, despite minor worries such as these, the doubles game at Rugby Fives is one of the most enjoyable recreations it is possible to find. Everything is so confined and intimate, that the players, all four of them defending the same area, present an appearance more like four people playing together than two teams divided against each other. Perhaps this is

the secret of the popularity of these court games, where player
and opponent are called upon to defend the same territory.
Such conditions make sociability imperative and it is easier
to admire an opponent who stands with you facing the same
objective than one who is attacking in the opposite direction.

Whatever be the reason, the grim silence that so often is a
feature of both players and spectators of other games is
entirely absent from the Fives court during doubles play.
The rallies can be tense and silent enough, but their climax
is usually greeted with a shout from one or other of the players.
Four people are rarely in a Fives court for long without something amusing happening to one of them, and the fact that
players as well as spectators have time to see that it is amusing
makes Fives in every way a game.

All the rules of the singles game which have been dealt
with above apply to the doubles game with certain additions,
but wherever applicable the words ' server ', or ' striker ',
' opponent ' or ' player ' should in the doubles game be taken
to include his partner.   Thus, when the ruling says that the
server may take the striker's blackguard providing he shouts
' Taken ' before he plays his shot, it will also apply to the
server's partner.

Facing the front wall, the server stands on the left-hand side
of the court, about half-way between the back and the front
wall, except when he is actually serving the ball, as will be
explained later. His partner stands diagonally opposite to
him in the right-hand corner. The striker and his partner
take up the contrary positions near the right-hand side wall
and the left-hand back corner respectively.   For the purpose of
playing the doubles game an imaginary line is drawn from
the centre of the front wall to the centre of the back wall, so
dividing the court into two equal halves. The server and the
striker's partner defend the left-hand half, while the striker
and the server's partner guard the right-hand half of the
court. We shall see when we come to discuss variations of the
Rugby Fives game, such as Winchester Fives, that this division
is not always practised, but for the absolutely plain Rugby
court without a buttress of any kind, this plan is generally
adhered to and is recommended as most satisfactory. The
line down the centre being quite imaginary, there is naturally
no hard-and-fast rule about taking balls on your partner's
side of the court, and much of the skill of a good doubles player
depends upon his judgment of when, and when not, to change

E

sides. Should he change his partner will immediately cross
over to prevent confusion and thus avoid the necessity of
allowing lets which will always occur if constant changing is
permitted.

In the preliminary rally of the doubles game all four players
take part to decide who is to be server or which side is ' up '.
The server and his partner are known as ' hands ', first hand
in, second hand in, so that the abbreviated form of scoring,
' 5—3 seconds ', would mean five points to three, second hand
in. The server remains ' in ' until his side loses a rally, when
his second hand or partner becomes server, but when the
side again loses a rally, their opponents serve. Thus, if the
score stood at ' 5—3 second hand in ' and the serving side
lost the rally, the score would become ' 3—5 first hand in '
and so on. The side, however, which wins the preliminary
rally, and becomes the serving side, has, at that time, only
one hand.

The side that is ' down ', the striking side, must change
strikers after every point scored by their opponents. Incidentally, it may here be noted that there is much difference
of opinion concerning the popularity of this rule. Tradition
at many schools and clubs supports the practice of changing
strikers after every two points lost, while some teams never
change their strikers at all. The Rugby Fives Association
were, of course, obliged to make some ruling on this vexed
subject, and naturally whatever decision they arrived at was
bound to oppose the wishes of a large number of players.
Probably it will not matter a great deal if tradition remains
too strong for this rule, as long as teams can come to an
amicable arrangement and as long as the clubs and schools
concerned will be content to play competitions under the
ruling to which they are unaccustomed. As a personal and
biased opinion I should say that there is a great deal to be
said for changing strikers at every two points instead of one,
because it gives a better sense of stability to the striking side ;
but for leaving the striker unchanged until he becomes server
there is nothing to be said, for a good server matched against
a weak striker can win the match almost without their partners
touching the ball, which seems rather ridiculous when you
consider that it is called a game of doubles.

The constant changing of strikers, the going ' up ' and
' down ', the two ' hands ', all accumulate to make doubles
play a little bewildering, especially if there should be no

umpire. Mistakes, therefore, will arise generally following an unusually long rally. Thus, if the wrong player serves or strikes, the mistake must be pointed out before the end of the rally, otherwise the rally counts ; " but at the next ' hand ', the pairs shall revert to their correct order ".

The server only, and not his partner, may take the striker's return of service, but in the case of a blackguard either the server or his partner may take it.

That, in brief, is all that there is to say concerning how the game of Rugby Fives is played both in singles and doubles. There can be little difference of opinion now that the rules of the Association have been published. But what remains is to tell how to play the game, and on that subject everyone is entitled to his own judgment. Accordingly I shall confine myself as much as possible to elementary points of the game about which there can be no controversy, and when I come to deal with tactics I shall make suggestions which are in agreement with my own experience, but which are not necessarily any better than the tactics adopted by other players.

In the following pages it will become clearer why so many people prefer the doubles game to that of singles. In doubles the ability of a player cannot be negatived by the superior physical fitness of his opponent. In singles it can. Indeed, one of the most certain methods of winning a single and one which I shall recommend is to keep your opponent on the run, should you be in a position to do so. You have to have ability and command of a variety of shots as well as a good wind to do this, but you may still be an inferior player to your opponent and yet win. In doubles the out-manœuvring of your opponents can only be achieved by skill and court craft ; it is useless to attempt to run them off their feet.

CHAPTER TEN

RUGBY FIVES (*continued*)

BY JOHN ARMITAGE

HOW TO PLAY THE GAME

FIVES is rather a dull game to practise alone, and only the very young or the very keen enter a court to hit a ball around by themselves. This is a pity, for much can be learnt about the art of the game by the smallest amount of time spent in this way. Learning by match play is, of course, the best experience of all, but in the excitement and hurry of a match, it is not often easy to see the potentialities of a new shot, which a little quiet reflection in a court by oneself would bring. You will never learn to play Fives by practising alone, but you will learn how to play.

Fives, again, is not an altogether easy game to explain, for although it is simplicity itself as regards ruling and gear, it is also rather vague. Probably it is because it has never, until now, been a subject of much publicity, that it has not evoked anything like a complete jargon of its own, which leaves the writer with a paucity of terms to explain his meaning. Other games have a particular name for every stroke that is played, Fives does not. Actually a Fives player, since he has no racket to play about with, can never make a stroke in the accepted sense of the term, but merely hits the ball with his hand and makes a 'shot'. Moreover, a Fives player will not refer to these shots in a language of technical terms that only another Fives player may understand, but will say that so-and-so made a 'great shot' or even that he 'flicked the ball from off the back wall, so that it just nicked the corner', but he will not so much as refer to the 'drop-shot', although he will frequently see it played, unless he happens to be a player of Squash Rackets as well. In what follows I shall probably be tempted to borrow from time to time the language of other games to explain my meaning, but I shall be careful that it does explain, and not confuse the reader who is interested in Rugby Fives alone.

68

As in all other games, the making of a good Fives player depends on cultivating good habits from the very start. This is difficult, for the novice invariably finds that for the time being he is more successful with his bad habits than with the good. It is always a difficult task to sacrifice present enjoyment to future proficiency, but there are one or two early pitfalls that to step into is suicide. In most games it is the correct grip of the racket, or whatever implement it is that you are using, that at first seems awkward ; in Fives, the hindrance is much greater, it is the obligation of using the left or the other arm. In dealing with this subject I shall assume that my player is by nature right-handed, but if he should be left, he will please read right for left in the ensuing context.

Taking for granted that the player has already been in a Fives court once or twice, that he has a vague notion of what is expected of him, and has learnt to hit the ball with some consistency (and even this is not so easy as it may look to the uninitiated), then, if he is right-handed, he has probably only learnt to hit the ball with his right hand and a straight arm as well. A novice at Fives will usually find that his left arm is useless ; he has never needed to employ it at any other game and he is finding it quite difficult enough to hit the ball above the board with his right hand. If he is not very strong-minded, he will for the time being give up trying to use it, and as his right hand improves he will be more and more loath to start again at the beginning, and it is a harder beginning, with his left. The deceit and treachery of the business is, that playing with other novices, who also prefer not to use their left hands, he will not at first find it much of a handicap, for the pace will be slow, making it possible for him to run round almost everything and take it with his right. Of course, there will be the occasional and miraculous shot from his opponent that will cling to the side wall, and this he must leave, or flattening himself against the wall, scoop up a return with his right hand. Winchester and Eton Fives players learn to use their left hands more quickly because of the buttress on the left-hand side wall, but whereas the former become really ambidextrous, the latter employ the left hand very little except for the volley.

No Fives player can avoid using his left hand a little, for he must learn to return the striker's first cut—an Eton Fives expression which I must beg the use of—but it is extraordinary how many people will make shift with the minimum of proficiency in this respect, and how well some of them succeed with their

tactics of flattening themselves against the wall and hoping for
the best. The worst offenders are left-handed players who have
no right hand. Since they strike on the left-hand corner and
receive the first cut of the right-handed player on the left-hand
side wall, they have no experience of playing with their right
hands, unless they seek it. Then comes the day when they are
obliged to play a single against another left-handed player.
This is providentially seldom, for the result is lamentable. The
game will take most of the afternoon, for neither is able to return
with his right hand the strong first cut of his opponent. Fives
can be played quite successfully by these one-handed exponents,
but they have such definite limitations that they can never hope
to achieve more than an average good standard.

The first ambition of every Fives player should be, therefore,
to learn to use both hands equally well, and the second to
employ his wrists with every shot. A man who plays with a
straight arm can never be more than good ; he cannot develop
that accuracy and finesse of touch which comes from a flick of
the wrist ; he cannot obtain that little extra pace off the walls
or floor which deceives the opponent, and, most important of all,
he cannot conceal the direction of his shot. At all times he is
an open player, whose every movement betrays his immediate
intention, while more often than not he is clumsy and a nuisance
to everybody in the court.

If you will glance at the illustrations you will see that the
arms of the players either about to play a shot, or having made
it, are raised not very high, while the arms of the other players
are hanging loosely at their sides. This is important. The arm
should always be loose and flexible, in much the same way, if
this conveys anything to anyone, as one is taught to hold the
arm when learning to play the pianoforte. The arm is controlled but supple. There is not a single shot in Rugby Fives,
except an occasional jab volley which will be dealt with later on,
which should be played without a movement of the wrist. The
strength of a shot comes naturally enough from the arm, but
the leverage and control of pace from the wrist and fingers.
Flick your wrist and fingers as you would play a shot, and you
will see how foolish it is to talk of Fives as though it were
played with the palm of the hand alone.

I am not going to spend much time in discussing body
balance, a good eye, and all those other attributes which a man
will find to be essential, if he is to be good at any game that is
played with a flying ball. Natural fitness and physical qualities

are all as valuable to the Fives player as to the exponent of any other sport, perhaps more so, for in Fives every muscle is called into play, while the left side of the body should be exercised as much as the right. Briefly then, when playing a straight up-and-down shot on the right the balance of your body should be thrown on the left foot, which you move across to the ball, watching the ball carefully all the time ; similarly, the balance is on the right foot when playing a shot on the left. This is a good general rule but by no means without exception ; the novice would do well to follow it. Plate XVI is a good example of this. The player has taken the ball with his right hand and aimed for the left-hand corner. As he struck the ball he threw the balance of his body on to the left foot and at the com-pletion of the shot, as the position of his right foot shows, he was perfectly poised and thus enabled to time and place the ball to the best advantage. The other photographs illustrate the same point ; the balance resting on the left or right foot.

  Placing is, of course, all-important but it cannot be taught, as it is part of what is termed ' court craft ', that is an instinct for position, knowing where the ball is, where it should go next, and where you should stand to receive it. Court craft is the fruit of experience. To keep your eye on the ball is of chief importance, instinct will soon tell you where the top of the board is and how to find the angles you want. It cannot tell you how to make your objective ; only practice can do that.

  Everyone who is ambitious will try to run before he can walk, and Fives has many attractive shots which will appeal to the novice before he has mastered the simplest stroke. He should try to avoid this. There is nothing that is so well repaid as absolute concentration for a long period on the most elementary shots, for they serve not only as a basis for all future develop-ment, but as scoring and defensive strokes for the whole of a Fives career.

  Once you have learnt to hit the ball with either hand, the next matter on which you must concentrate is to hit the ball low and to a length. There is no necessity to weary yourself trying to hit hard, as speed will come of its own accord as you gain better control over your limbs and wrists. Besides, hitting hard, if it is more than an inch or two above the board, is value-less, for the ball will rebound easily for your opponent from off the back wall. Controlling the length of your shot is the more difficult accomplishment, for under modern conditions, when courts still differ in size, a player must learn this lesson by experience. Constant practice on the same court will soon give you an excellent basis on which to calculate the differences of others, but a length on a foreign court is always difficult to command, for courts even if they should tally in measurement will generally differ in speed because of their surface composition. If you play your Fives on a court that has no back wall, the necessity for commanding a perfect length loses its supreme importance, but with a back wall the slightly overhit ball will ' sit up ' and present an easy shot to your opponent, for although the novice is shy of allowing anything to reach the back, it is the favourite hunting-ground of the experienced player.

A player, then, must hit low and he must hit to a length ; thirdly, he must learn to control the side walls. Every beginner has a natural desire to play for the corners, which are so much more exciting, and to neglect the straight up-and-down shots along the side walls. If he does so, he will not only throw away point after point by hitting the ball down, but he will be eliminating from his game the most valuable shot that there is, for the controlled shot that clings to the side wall is or should be the basic play for all players, and by controlled, I mean that the ball is hit to a length, so that it will reach but not rebound from the back wall. Over and over again have I seen a point thrown away by a player, who having worked his opponent out of position, uses the cross-shot and brings him up again ready to kill the ball into the far corner. However it is hit, a ball that is clinging to the side wall is extremely hard to return with any dexterity, and the player may well hope to be able to put away the next shot with the whole court at his mercy. The best advice is to learn to play controlled side-wall shots from any position and especially to flick the ball down the left-hand wall with the left wrist when still facing towards your front. These shots will not only enable you to keep your opponent on the run, but will afford you splendid respite when you are hard pressed.

To the novice the back wall presents many difficulties ; he is afraid of it, which is curious, for when he is practised he will look upon it as his one sure guide. In every ball game the player has not only to obtain a mastery over his opponent but over the ball itself. In Rugby Football the bounce of the ball when you are following up may determine the chances of a try, in Eton Fives it is the antics of the ball after it has hit the various obstacles which lie in its path. The back wall in Rugby Fives is something like that ; it bewilders, and the novice is never

THE BACK WALL.

Top : " IN NINE CASES OUT OF TEN, IF THE PLAYER IS A BEGINNER, HE SHOULD GO TO MEET IT."
(PAGE 73.)

Bottom : THE ATTACKING PLAYER WILL ALWAYS CHOOSE TO FOLLOW THE BALL ROUND. (PAGE 74.)

Plates XVIII & XIX

quite certain whether he should chase round the corner after the ball, or run to meet it in the opposite direction. He is unaccustomed to a back wall which enables his opponent to attack him in the rear, and further, as it demands much bending, twisting and turning, and hitting the ball from seeming awkward positions, he for a while dreads it. On the other hand, the experienced player, who knows what to expect and for whom full knees bend has no terrors—and incidentally the ability to bend and stoop easily is no small advantage in Rugby Fives, which is partly the reason why it is considered such an arduous game—regards the back wall as a rock upon which he can confidently place his trust. Every time he takes a ball from off the back wall, he knows exactly how far away he is from the front, at least he does on his own court, and he can drop the ball from there accurately on to the front wall. From anywhere else he has not that precise knowledge, and he has not the time to think, but off the back wall he does know and there is usually that split second of extra time that is all-important for making the best possible shot.

It has occurred to me that perhaps I generalize too freely concerning the stable feeling with which all practised Fives players regard the back wall. I do not think so, and if I do, it is because those who dislike it have failed to make full use of it. How to make full use of it is the question that must next command our attention. I said above that the novice is often bothered by back wall shots, because he cannot make up his mind whether he should follow the ball round or go to meet it. In nine cases out of ten, if the player is a beginner, he should go to meet it. That is to say, if the ball has been hit by his opponent in such a way that it will strike the left-hand side wall first and then the back wall, the player should approach the ball from the opposite direction to which it is coming and return it with his left hand. Similarly, if the ball strikes the right-hand side wall and then the back wall, he should place himself in such a position that he can return it easily with his right hand. If the ball is hit straight on to the front wall so that it rebounds direct to the back wall, it is permissible for the player to take it with either hand, so that he will generally elect to take it with his right, if there has been plenty of time for him to move so that he may easily do so.

It is true that if the novice pursues the ball round the angle instead of going to meet it, he will often make a better shot, should he get it up at all, than he would by taking it in the more

orthodox manner. This is an accident. By pursuing the ball
he has got into a better position by chance for hitting it, than he
would have done had he had more time to think. Most people
find it more or less easy to stand correctly when addressing the
ball which is in front of them, but the common mistake of all
beginners is to stand too near the side walls, so that they cramp
the action of their arms, and much too near the back wall.
That is why, when following the ball round, they sometimes
make a better shot, for when they find that they are not so near
as they could wish, they reach forward and play perfectly;
generally they miss it altogether. A player learns by experience
when to follow the ball round and when to go to meet it;
actually he will always choose to follow it round if he is an
attacking player, whenever he can, for in this way he increases
the speed of the game and gives his opponent less time to think.
This is quite an important consideration, but it should not be
forgotten that the player who swings for impossible shots around
the back corners for the sake of enlivening the game, is a nuisance and a danger, especially in doubles.

Now that we have generalized rather widely about the game,
taking notice of the difficulties, the use of walls and the points
to cultivate, let us go back to the beginning and consider the
actual shots a good player may be expected to know and utilize.
Since it is the server who begins a game, let us commence with
him. He can do nothing in service to help himself or his side, as
it is his duty to throw the ball up, as near as possible, in accordance with the striker's demands. Most strikers will request the
server to stand on the side of them nearest the wall, while he is
throwing the ball up, so that the angle at which the ball is
thrown may be a narrow one. This means that as soon as he
has thrown, the server must immediately cross to the other side
of the court in order to take the striker's return. Take a look
at Plate XV; it shows a view of the court just as a game is
about to commence. 1 and 3 are partners, as also are 2 and 4.
2 is the server and 1 the striker. 2 is about to throw the ball up
in the right-hand corner and he is standing behind and a little
to the right of 1. When he has thrown the ball up, he will
immediately cross the court to a position on the left of 3. In
the picture 3 and 4 are both standing too far forward, they
should be about a yard from the back wall, but they were moved
forward in order to be included in the photograph.

Most strikers have strong opinions about how the ball should
be thrown up, and these opinions differ enormously. Some will

prefer them high and soft, others low and far down the side wall, while every other combination that it is possible to think of has its advocates. Most, however, are agreed to have the ball thrown at a narrow angle, as this enables the striker to find the nick of the corner should he so desire. By all means have the ball served just as you wish it, and by all means try every variety of way until you have discovered which will suit you best, but do not demand such wearisome accuracy that the server must have three or four attempts to throw the ball up before he satisfies you completely ; it is a poor player who can make nothing of anything but the very best.

There is a curious lack of variety about some strikers' return of service or first cut, which is strange as it is one of the most important features of the game. They seem to imagine that ' cracking ' the ball into the corner at the same speed and at the same angle on every occasion is all that is required of them, and that it is then that they begin to play. Now and again they strike an absurdly short one, that can deceive no one, as it is a pat from the hand rather than a stroke played from the wrist. Every striker should be able to keep the server guessing when he plays his first cut, even if he can do no more. That is the inherent value of the first cut, and the best use that can be made of it is not to vary the kind of shot so much as its speed. You will find that nothing will bother the server so much as returns of service that disguise their speed. The speeds should not vary greatly but constantly. All this is a matter of practice for the striker, but there is a variety of first cuts which he will do well to use at intervals. Generally, I consider it best to adopt one kind of return and trust to the variations of speed to bewilder my opponent, still it is a good idea at the beginning of a game to try a little variety, for you may discover one particular return that the server cannot manage.

The shot which might well be called the ordinary first cut, hits the right side wall near the corner, the front wall a little farther from the corner but close to the top of the board, and then comes across to about the centre of the left-hand wall. I should explain perhaps in case it should cause confusion, that I use the expression ' first cut ' simply because it is serviceable and not as an Eton Fives player would use it, because he makes this first stroke with his hand aslant and a downward motion. It is not possible in Rugby Fives to get much cut on the ball with any success. This ordinary first cut is hit by the striker quite easily from about 10 feet away from the front wall and a little over a foot away from the right-hand side wall. The speed is varied by the amount of flick imparted from the wrist. There is, however, a diversity of first cuts that can be used, but which are more useful when played occasionally than when adopted as a regular stroke.

Among these is the shot that comes back unexpectedly to the server's right hand, and this is made by striking at a long narrow angle. The occasional short drop shot is also profitable, for it will bring the server up the court and out of position, while there is always a good chance, if you conceal it well enough, that he will fail to reach it altogether. A flick of the wrist will do this, but you must be careful to approach the ball each time in the same manner, or the server will guess your purpose. Two other returns of service are sometimes successful. One is hitting the ball almost square on to the side wall about 4 feet from the corner, so that it rebounds on to the facing wall in the opposite corner of the court, and striking the left-hand side wall, comes back across very nearly to the spot where it first started from. The other is to hit the ball very hard and very high, so that having struck the corner near the roof and the opposite side wall it bounces finally somewhere in the neighbourhood of the back right-hand corner. This is quite a valuable shot in doubles play, now that the server's partner is unable to return the striker's first cut, for by his position he will frequently impede the efforts of the server to reach the ball. But for that very reason it is not a good or popular shot, as there is an element of unfairness in it and it should be used seldom except as a means of enlivening a dull game.

Corner shots across the face of the front wall, whether from right to left or left to right, should be used infrequently, especially in doubles play. Unless they are very accurately and carefully played they will bounce away from the centre of the front wall and present an easy ' smash ' to an opponent, while even if they do not, they are likely to bring the opponent into a good position. In singles they are best played from the back of the court, either when your opponent is right up in front hoping to volley your return, when an angle shot may surprise and pass him ; or when your opponent is boxed in a corner behind you, when you may either drop the ball in the top opposite angle and hope to put away his next easy return, or sensing the direction in which he is preparing to run, you make a cross-shot the reverse way. The most usual situation when a cross-shot is employed is shown in Plate

XVI. The player on the right, having worked his opponent down the left-hand wall, has received an easy return and he is shown in the photograph at the completion of his stroke, the ball travelling across the face of the court and bouncing just in front of him, after hitting the left-hand corner. The player on the left is now a long way from the ball, so that even if he reaches it, he will probably make a poor return which his opponent will kill down the left-hand side wall.

In doubles it is best to be chary of angle shots altogether and especially of those that cross the face of the front wall ; there are now two opponents to contend with, and one of them should always be in a position to smash. The best use one can make of the angles in doubles play is for varying the speed. A ball hit very sharply into the corner with a flick of the wrist will come back very quickly, and there is a good chance that the player who is in the front of the court will try and return it and hit it down. Another effective corner shot is made with the hand nearest the side wall. The player should have the appearance of one about to return the ball either straight back along the side wall or across court, instead with a turn and a flick of the wrist the ball strikes the side wall first and glances across the face of the front wall. If the player in Plate XVI had done this he might have caught his opponent running across when it was too late to turn back. Nor should the reverse corner shot be neglected. On this occasion the ball hits the front wall first and then the side wall, and although this shot is rarely as we say a ' winner ', it is a useful change and might catch your adversary on the wrong foot.

But to my mind the best and most exhilarating shot of this kind is one that is comparatively easy to do and which will invariably turn defence into attack. Your opponent has placed his shot down the left-hand wall ; it is not clinging to that wall, but it is near enough for him to expect you to take it with your left hand, so he moves to the right side in case you should hit hard across, knowing that if you should hit down the left side wall, it will not be a fast one, and he will have time to move back and take it. If the ball comes round just sufficiently, as it often will, instead of doing either of these shots which he expects, you pivot round on your foot and with your right hand drop the ball into the top right-hand corner as near to the top of the board as you possibly can. It is a shot which demands great accuracy of touch, but there is usually plenty of time and if you are lucky you will play it just at that moment when your opponent is looking round, hoping that you have missed it. In Plate XVII the player is attempting this shot in a doubles match. If he is accurate he will probably win the point, for both his opponents are standing well back and have turned to watch him.

There is a great diversity of opinion among Rugby Fives players concerning the potentialities of the volley, and except as a quick scoring stroke on special occasions, some will not admit its value at all. But here, I think, we can learn a little from the game of Eton Fives—as the players of that game could learn a good deal from Rugby Fives if they would admit it— for the judicious use of the volley will gain its exponent many points and an invaluable amount of breathing space besides. It is sometimes worth while to throw away an early point if you make your opponent exhaust himself in gaining it, and although the few volleys that you put in at the start may not tire him completely, they will weary him in comparison, and you may then push home your advantage.

Over and over again have I seen a Winchester Fives player defeat a Rugby Fives player in a Rugby court because he exploited the volley. The volley figures much more prominently in the Winchester game for reasons that will be obvious when we come to discuss it later on, but that is no excuse for the Rugby Fives player who is completely nonplussed when he sees it in action. The volley should be used in Rugby Fives only when occasion demands and not indiscriminately. Wild volleying is worthless, but to volley well is both neat and effective. To be effective a volley must be close to the board and accurately placed, and as the ball is usually taken overhead, it necessitates clean hitting with a dropping wrist as the arm comes forward. Much practice must be expended on this shot before it becomes in any way perfect, for the ball tends to fly high or straight on to the ground. Overhead volleying should not be indulged in, unless the player is very adept, or caught in a tight corner.

The volley from a straight left arm is used by some people. It sweeps the ball right across court and is an ugly shot, but useful for obtaining a ' breather ', or changing the direction of the attack. The volley, too, is a fine counter-attack to the lob, especially if you are able to pick the ball from off the side walls. This is most difficult and I have only known one player who could do it well, and he, although brilliant, was not dependable. Unless you have a natural preference for the volley, I feel it is wise to content yourself with using it for fast attacking shots that approach you waist high, or for a sudden jab into the corner to put the ball out of reach of your opponent to win the point. But the Rugby Fives player must be able to volley, for it alone will get him out of many awkward situations, save his breath when he is tired, while there are some first cuts, which he will find it impossible to return, unless he has that stroke at his command.

The half-volley does not present many difficulties, if you have a fast enough eye to do it at all. It is a useful shot providing you can apply it well and it should be used either as a fast attacking stroke or for lobbing. But remember that a weak half-volley is the easiest prey of all to an opponent. I have said that the half-volley can be used for lobbing and it is to that very vexed question of this art which we must now turn.

To my mind lobbing is bad for any game and should be used purely as a defensive stroke to get you out of an immediately difficult position. If it is used frequently, as it may well be and is by good exponents, the game becomes uninteresting, the opponent grows tired and exasperated, and the result, although it may be a win for you, is undeserved. I shall refer again to this matter shortly. The lob may be used to check the man who consistently occupies the front of the court and attempts to volley all your returns. It may be used advantageously high down the side walls to gain you a moment or two's brief respite during a long rally. There, I feel, its utility ends, or at least its desirability, but whether you agree with this or not, depends entirely on what attitude you adopt towards games.

Happily or unhappily, that is all that can be said concerning the actual stroke play of Rugby Fives. It is not a game that lends itself to a scientific description. Every shot played is different from the next and must be treated on its own peculiar merits. Most balls are returned too quickly for the player to position his body perfectly on each occasion, and to be successful he must learn to hit accurately, however he is placed. He must learn, too, to be a remarkably good judge of distance, for in the course of a match it will be rare for him to play two shots that coincide exactly in distance from the side and front walls. That is why he is glad to allow the ball to reach the back wall ; its distance from the front is known. Speed is another factor that the player must take into consideration. For should the actual distance be the same, the pace at which the ball is travelling alters the apparent space between him and the front wall.

That is, the ' touch ' is changed, and ' touch ' is both distance and speed, which is the only criterion by which a Fives player need judge. The variety of play, then, is supplied not by the number of shots that it is possible to play, but by the diversity of the shots themselves. There is no settled school of play, and as a result there is a marked individuality among all players, so that it is difficult to point to any particular person whose style one would do well to follow. The best players, one may feel sure, hit beautifully low and to a consistent length, two degrees of excellence which allow them to take the initiative, which after all is the first step to victory.

We must turn now to match play and the best tactics we can adopt if we wish to win our single or a game of doubles. And in the first place something which applies to them both, and at the chance of sounding foolish, a word of caution. Get really warm before the serious business of the match begins. The best way to do this is to play a few points gently among yourselves, as the exertion of running about will enliven your circulation and warm your hands better than knocking the ball up to one another or beating your gloved hands against the wall. It is suicide to attempt to play before you are warm, and yet in nine cases out of ten, a match will begin with one or other of the sides in this condition. Usually it is the visiting side, which, arriving late at the courts when the home team has been knocking up for about ten minutes, agrees to start immediately. Their hands are cold, and as a result they lose the first games in either court. There is no other method of getting warm except by knocking up beforehand, unless you choose to follow the example of certain foolhardy people, who warm and soften their hands in hot water before the start. If you do this, your hand will be a mass of bruises, as it will be if you begin cold, and the rest of the season will be a misery to you.

It is wise in singles play, if your opponent looks physically better proportioned than yourself, or is known to be in better training, to try and entice him to run about a bit during the early stages of the game, by making good use of the side walls and the occasional short drop shot. At the same time you must be careful that these tactics do not cause you to run about still more, as they sometimes do without your being aware of it. But if you are successful in doing this, you will probably be a point or two behind your opponent, and this is all to the good, for you must not neglect the psychological effect of your strategy. When he has tired a little you should make your effort and no matter what it costs you, try to score five points in a row. The demoralizing result upon your opponent, who has been winning 5-3 and a few minutes later is losing 8-5, is all-important, and is calculated to go a long way to giving you the match.

As soon as your opponent realizes that he cannot prevent you from keeping him on the run, he should resort to lobbing, in order to give himself time to breathe and regain confidence. A great deal will depend upon his execution of lobs, for if they do not throw you out of your stride, he will be caught in two minds and this should give you victory. But a match is never lost or won until the last point has been played, and once you begin to grow inaccurate, your opponent may produce a bigger variety of shots than those with which you can cope. Now, if you can, you should work your way consistently to the front of the court and volley his returns away, as this will help to rest you and possibly upset his calculations.

Nobody, of course, can do more than make suggestions for singles play. All players set about their game in their own way, working to get their opponent in such a position that their own favourite shots may meet with success. Few Fives players have a plan of campaign in their heads when they enter the court, but rather while they are still winning they play their shots as the opportunity presents itself. It is not until they are faced with defeat that they turn their attention to prevent their opponent from playing his. Possibly this is not the best method to adopt if you wish to win your match ; they might do better if they played throughout on the supposition that they were losing. Nevertheless, these are the tactics which I should like to recommend, for good and attractive Fives is the result and for the attacking player the game is its own reward.

Doubles are quite another matter. It is the combination of two partners that wins the match, not the merits of two individuals. Good combination is the result of much practice which enables the one to get, not so much accustomed to the play of the other, although this is important, as to think of himself in terms of the other ; that is, thinking automatically as a team and not as two individuals. The difficulty presented by such a situation is obvious. It means that frequently you must play shots which you would not otherwise have done, because such a stroke may benefit your partner. With a partner you must think much further ahead, and the next shot but one must be always in mind. Naturally, in singles you must think ahead

F

and in just the same way, but in order to do that you need only
be a judge of your own capabilities and this is not so difficult as
to estimate the ability of your partner. And further, some of
your best shots must be restricted because they may upset friend
and foe alike. There is nothing more annoying than to lose a
point by hitting your partner full pitch, because you have not
sensed his position. He will be annoyed also.

The key man in doubles play is the weakest member of the
four. His is a most responsible position, and he can, if he is
clever although weak, turn it to good account. The weakest
member of the four usually finds himself suffering from an un-
merciful and severe bombardment in the left-hand corner of the
court, from which his partner can do little to relieve him. All
will now depend upon two things—his ability to keep the ball
going with some variation of placing, and his partner's temperament. For once the latter begins to dash about the court,
taking balls that do not belong to him, the game is lost, for he
will lose as many points as his fellow.

'Poaching', as it is called, rarely meets with much success,
even if the one player is so much better than the others that he is
prepared to play single-handed against his opponents. I have
seen this practised, especially at schools, many times, when the
captain has given his partner instructions to keep out of the way.
The game that results is frightful, for the poor wretched weak-
ling rushes from corner to corner, conceding lets wherever he
goes, earning nothing but black looks from all sides. The best
plan is to allow the weak man to play his own game, although
encouraging him to change the direction of his attack as much
as possible. If he does not, he will be participating constantly
in an unequal struggle, a duel between his feeble left hand and
his antagonist's strong right, for obviously the latter will not be
disposed to change his tactics. It is a hard task to be expected
to concentrate all one's energy on changing the direction of the
attack, but this is what the fourth player must do if he wishes
to help his side. Psychologically, if he has any self-respect at
all, he will be tempted to continue hitting back at his tormentor,
but as this is exactly what is expected of him, he will do best in
every way to avoid doing so. It is no disgrace on these occasions
to admit your opponent to be a better player than yourself, and
to try and win by court craft, what you cannot hope to win by
skill.

However, it is not always good fortune to have two opponents
of unequal prowess. Faced with such a situation, it is most

natural to ply the weaker of the two with difficult shots, which are all, because of his weakness, supposed to be ' winners '. But even the veriest rabbit can upset calculations such as these. He will, for instance, play a great deal better than if he were neglected, or only called upon to play his fair share of the game. Further, he will do nothing that is expected of him ; sometimes he will miss the simplest shots and then play brilliantly ; he will mishit shot after shot, getting them up so awkwardly that his opponent will be caught on the wrong foot and out of position. But these are minor advantages, for his greatest achievement has been to cause his opponents to play an unthinking and foolish game, believing that they have only to hit the ball to win a point.

The ideal combination for a doubles team is, of course, a right-handed player who has also a good left hand, playing with a left-handed player who can use his right effectively. Such combinations are rare, but when two such players do come together, as there are two or more examples to be seen to-day, they present a most formidable opposition. To play against them is like attacking a machine, left or right it is all the same, for there is little chance of finding them out of position and points must be won by the placing and concealed speed of the shot, which may cause them to mishit the ball. Left- and right-handed players who are partners, usually remain each on one side during the match, except when the rules of service demand otherwise, after which they will change as soon as it is permissible. For instance, the right-handed player when he is serving must wait for the striker's first cut on the left-hand side of the court, but as soon as he has returned the ball, he will cross to the right-hand side. The usual combination is naturally two right-handed players, and both will defend the left-hand side as it falls to their lot. For this reason, they are practised, and are a better pair as a rule than the left- and right-handed players, who are more or less one hand short. One hand short, because as I have stated elsewhere, the left-handed player rarely makes use of his other arm.

The advantage that the left- and right-handed players have as partners, if they are not both ambidextrous, is mainly over inexperienced opponents, for it is the confusion that they are capable of which helps them to victory. The left-handed player striking in one corner and the right-handed partner striking in the other, is liable to confound the novice to such an extent that he loses all sense of position. He is perplexed and his game spoilt. It should perhaps be easier for him to receive the first cut of the left-handed player in the right-hand corner, but he does not find it so, because he is not sure where he should stand, and because it is a physical attribute of most left-handed players to be able to strike the ball harder than the ordinary player, as the left-handed batsman at cricket can so often be relied upon to punish the bowling. But such partners, left-handed and right-handed playing together, frequently leave themselves open to a most easy shot, which is often a ' winner ', the shot straight down the middle. If it is used judiciously, either they will both leave it to the other, or both attempt to play it, and in either case you have won the point. Such partners lack combination.

The whole art of doubles play is summed up in that one word, combination. To be successful, two players have got to combine to such an extent that they not only act as one man, but think as one man, and this can only be achieved by constant practice together. The shots for both singles and doubles are identically the same, only some are used more advantageously in the one than the other. The short quick volley is more useful in doubles, since one man is always in the front of the court to seize his opportunity, but the lob should be found more valuable in a single, for there is not, then, another opponent waiting behind to kill, should it be less than perfect. But to combine, that is the essence of the game, and to do this well implies getting the best not only out of yourself, but out of your partner. When he finds it necessary to cross the court there should be no shouting of " Change " ; you should quietly do the same, and he should know that you have done it. Always you should be ready to take anything your partner is unable to reach or deems it better to leave, and in doing this there should be no cries of " Yours " or " Mine ", words that indicate to your opponents that you are individuals and not a pair.

And now before I leave this section of my treatise, I wish to refer the reader back to my remarks concerning the art of lob-bing and to explain why I think that an injudicious practice of this stroke can ruin the whole game of Rugby Fives. It is a difficult and controversial question.

A man about to play a game must always, I take it, have two objects in view. One is to play the game as well as he can, the other to play so that he wins. The first is his duty to the game and himself, the second to his side. In many people's minds the two ideas may rightly tally, but it is not always so, and it is

not the case in Rugby Fives. Fortunately this criticism does
not often apply to doubles play, but a singles match is only too
frequently spoilt by the second of these considerations taking
precedence over the first. There is one method of winning a
single that is sometimes practised successfully, which depends
largely on the physical fitness of the player. Matched against
an opponent of superior ability, the player resorts to lobbing,
varying his game from time to time with short volleys into the
top corners. Unless the opponent is equally good at this kind
of play, which is unlikely, for he prides himself on his strokes, he
will get rattled, hit wildly and the match will be won. Now
from one point of view this is victory well won. Any other
tactics would have lost the match, and the player has shown
good strategy and a complete knowledge of the art of lobbing.
And lobbing is difficult, which if executed indifferently would
have lost him the game.

Is he to be congratulated ? Obviously for many reasons, yes,
but nevertheless his tactics have ruined the enjoyment of the
game, which has been boring for both sides, while the loser has
quite possibly lost his temper as well. He is quite definitely
still the better player of Rugby Fives, and yet he was unable to
win, simply because the winner has been content to get all his
good shots up and has perfected one stroke only, the lob. Or to
look at it from a different angle, the winner has been content not
to try and gain a point, but to wait until his opponent has lost
them all. It is a definite weakness of the game of Rugby Fives,
which the introduction of a buttress, however small, would at
once remove. But with it the buttress would remove something
else, which for many of us represents the real joy of Rugby Fives
and its superiority over all other forms of the game—its freedom.

We still profess to play our games for relaxation and amusement ; Rugby Fives, with its four walls and its no hazards of
any kind, has its stronghold in this idea. There is nothing in
Rugby Fives to balk the player except the merit of his opponent ;
luck is almost entirely eliminated and it is hardly possible for
the game to be held up because the ball has been hit out of
court, and this I humbly submit, for a game which gives the
maximum of exercise, is ideal. It is not the memory of an
individual win that lingers in the mind of a Rugby Fives player,
nor of individual prowess of any kind ; it is the game itself. This
is no attempt to glorify the players ; the same men play other
games and bow to the worries that that game demands. To-
day, it is needful to learn that we spend our time reading and

practising our games not that we may win more easily, but that
we may enjoy them more widely and more whole-heartedly.
It is a merit of Rugby Fives, that it lays no obstacle in the path
of such enjoyment, for it is the least exasperating of all games.
With that I must conclude my description of how the game
of Rugby Fives is played. I can only hope that somewhere
among the pages will be found some helpful indications of how
to play, and for the rest it has not been found to be too dull
reading. There remains to consider, however briefly, some
interesting variations of the game. Of these, Winchester Fives
is the only one that can be said to have anything more than a
purely local appeal, and I shall accordingly direct the bulk of
my attention to it. I would not have it believed that for that
reason I despise the forms of the game played elsewhere—nothing could be more untrue—but they all differ so minutely one
from the other, that to describe them all, even if I were capable
of such a thing, would both take too long and be irksome to the
reader. Sufficient to state here, that in general principles, they
agree.

CHAPTER ELEVEN

RUGBY FIVES (continued)

BY JOHN ARMITAGE

VARIATIONS OF THE GAME

IT is almost true to say, or it was a year or two ago, that no two sets of courts are identically the same. Nor do they differ, as a rule, in small unessential details, such as the position of the door, or the facing material of the walls. The differences concern much more prominent features of the court than that. It is the height, the breadth or the length, or still worse the height of the board from the floor. And as for the back wall, it might well be anything from 15 feet to 4, or absent altogether.

We can blame no one for this. As has been mentioned before, until recently there were no regulations regarding the proper construction of a Fives court, and courts were built either to the whim of a particular man or the amount of space available for their site. Indeed, to see some courts, one might well be pardoned for believing that when no more funds for their erection were forthcoming, the builder ceased to build, and the result was called a Fives court.

Many courts have no back wall at all, similar in that respect to an Eton court, but whereas the Eton court has a protecting buttress and ledges to keep the ball in play, the plain Rugby Fives court without one is at a sad disadvantage. Some courts make up for the loss of the back wall by a small buttress on the left-hand side wall, but this compensates but little for the loss of variety which only a back wall can supply. Before the Association fixed the height of the back wall at 6 feet, walls of 10 feet and walls of 4 or 5 feet were the most usual. The reason for this was a practical one. If the court had a spectators' gallery, it was natural to build it about 10 feet from the ground, well out of harm's way, and as a result the players took the opportunity to use the whole of that height as ' in play '. If there was no spectators' gallery the wall had to be low, in order that the

audience outside could peer through the protecting wire.
There is this to be said for the old style of court, the players had
the benefit of any amount of fresh air. But short back walls
are annoying, because the ball can bounce from the floor more
than 4 feet in height and frequently does, and high back walls
encourage the lob and loose hitting. Altogether the new ruling
may be said to be very satisfactory.

The most abbreviated style of court that I have ever seen and

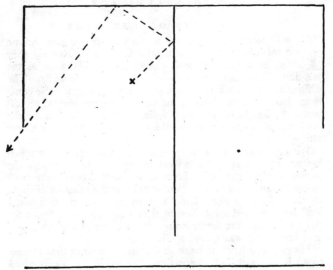

Fig. 5.

played in is constructed in pairs. They are, of necessity, open
to the air and consist of a front wall and an ordinary-length side
wall, which runs down the middle. This side wall forms the
right-hand side wall of the left-hand court and left-hand side
wall of the right-hand court. The two remaining side walls on
the outside of either court are of the same height as the middle
wall, but only half its length. There is no back wall, but the
floor area, which is considered to be in play, extends about 3
feet beyond the middle and dividing wall, as can be seen in the
accompanying illustration.

As may be imagined, a curious game results, in which volley-ing plays an unusually large part. There is one stroke which is particularly exciting. If you should happen to hit the middle side wall in just such a position, that the ball will strike the front wall and then the opposite side wall, at the point where it has been cut short, as it is quite easy to do, your opponent, or if you happen to be the opponent, you, will be left with the option of leaving it and thus losing the point, or returning it with the risk of damaging your hand severely. Most people will elect to leave it, if they cannot volley it before it reaches the side wall, but it is a disheartening way of losing a point.

I shall mention only one other court before going on to des-cribe the game as it is played at Winchester. This is a complete Eton Fives court which is roofed in and has a Rugby Fives back wall. I have only seen this court and never played in it, but all who have, assure me that the game is most interesting, and I can well believe them, for a game of Eton Fives, when you can hit as hard as you like without fear of allowing the ball to go out of play, must be an exciting pastime. But here, perhaps, it is neither in place nor fair to describe other courts so eccentric in character and in local hazards that they demand local ruling to recompense the player for their peculiarity. Their strange construction can upset the best exponents of the game. But although unfamiliar conditions can be very annoying to the visiting side, I do submit that there is another and more humor-ous side to the question, and the fact that men should be ready to play in them in the lieu of something better is surely only another proof that nothing can deny the Rugby Fives player his game.

THE WINCHESTER GAME

It will be seen from the drawing on next page that Winchester Fives differs only in one particular from the ordinary Rugby Fives court, and that it differs even less from it than some other courts which nevertheless still retain the name of Rugby. But whereas those courts are but isolated examples, Winchester Fives has a considerable following among other schools and their game is played to some extent all over the country. And again, although the introduction of a buttress may in itself be only a small matter, the difference it makes to the play is considerable.

There is no reason why the measurements of a Winchester court should be different in any particular, except for the altera-tions caused by the buttress, from the measurements quoted above as suitable for a Rugby Fives court. Actually the courts at Winchester do differ slightly in length, being 27 feet 11 inches against 28 feet, and in front-wall breadth 17 feet 10 inches against 18 feet. The greatest difference, however, lies in the height of the back wall, which is 14 feet against 6.

To describe a Winchester Fives court as being similar to a Rugby Fives court except for the buttress on the left-hand side wall, is likely to be misleading. For the so-called buttress is in reality the point at which the court narrows sharply and not an

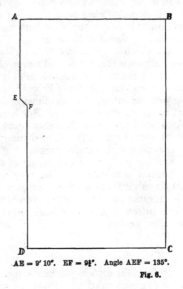

AE = 9′ 10″.   EF = 9¾″.   Angle AEF = 135°.

Fig. 6.

excrescence or support for the wall. From that point the wall maintains the same slightly narrower distance from the opposite side wall. However, for the sake of simplicity this projection is called universally the buttress. Here is a ground plan of the court.

As can be seen, the surface area of the buttress is of no great size, and yet the introduction of such a projection into a court entirely alters the tactics of the game. In the first place, a width of 9¾ inches, however small it may sound, is quite sufficient for a good Fives player to hit just as often as he pleases.

This means that if you are playing doubles, either you or your partner must be a constant guard to the buttress, watching in the front of the court for any ball that may rebound off it at whatever angle. Here we have a complete alteration in our positional arrangement of partners. In Rugby Fives it is customary for one player to guard the left-hand side of the court and the other the right, but in the Winchester game one player stands in the front of the court and returns absolutely everything that he can possibly reach, while his partner covers the whole of the back of the court, retrieving balls that the other has missed and returning lobs.

I am indebted to Mr. R. de W. K. Winlaw and his brother Mr. A. W. E. Winlaw, both of Winchester College, for much of the information contained in this article about their game. Most of my first-hand information about this sort of Fives has been gained by watching Wykehamists in a Rugby court adapting the tactics of their game to Rugby Fives, generally with marked success. Nevertheless, although I am exceedingly grateful for their help, I take naturally full responsibility for any remarks that are contained herein.

There is no doubt that the doubles game of Winchester Fives is a very fine sport, the introduction of the buttress supplying many interesting features that the plain Rugby court cannot hope to provide. Yet it must be admitted that what it gains in excitement, it loses in equality. The Rugby Fives player, whether he is serving or striking, is obliged to think of his partner as much as himself; the Winchester player is not. The Winchester player takes whatever he can, and leaves his partner only what he cannot reach or misses. This, although it is right in theory, really only applies to the best pairs, for until a player has mastered the volley, he will find it quite useless to stand in the middle of the court about 3 or 4 feet from the front wall, in which position volleying is about the only shot that can be employed. We will assume for the moment that we are dealing with a very good pair and that the two players A and B are playing together as partners. B is at the back of the court. He is an offensive and not defensive player, but his job at the moment is to get everything up and to work his opponents into a bad position, so that they will ultimately play a weak return, which A will be able to kill with a volley. A is standing in the front of the court about 3 or 3½ feet from the front wall. His object is to kill with the volley any ball that comes within his reach. To do this he must keep a watchful eye on the buttress, for if he allows a ball to hit it, he will have small chance from his position of making a good return. If the opponent has played a clinging shot to the left-hand wall, A will try and cut it off before it reaches the buttress, with a volley which is made with a flick of the wrist and which takes the ball straight off the face of the wall. It is one of the prettiest and neatest shots in Fives, and one over which the Winchester Fives player alone gains a mastery, for the Rugby Fives player deems it far wiser to allow the ball to rebound off the back wall. But as everyone knows, so much volleying has its less attractive side, for even the best players will only get the tips of their fingers to the ball sometimes, and nothing is more annoying to partner B than to see easy returns for him, lost, because A could not refrain from trying for them.

But if a good player will fail occasionally with his volleys from this position, anyone less than good cannot hope to succeed, and so inexperienced and less able pairs are advised to adopt quite different tactics for their game. Partner A, after he has thrown the ball up in service, will crouch under the front wall watching the buttress. This position is useless except for getting up returns that have hit the buttress, but at least he will not lose points. B is now the more important member of the pair, for besides having most of the work to do, he must be relied upon to make the winning strokes. Thus it is, if a good and a weak player are partnered together, the weak player will spend most of his time crouching under the front wall while the other plays the game, but at least this is more satisfactory than the weak partner's position in the Rugby game ; he is serving a useful purpose by watching the buttress and he is out of the way.

The more obvious differences, however, in Winchester Fives concern the server and striker. As in the Rugby game the striker may elect to take his first cut on the right- or left-hand corner, but whereas in that game it would make no difference to his chances of success, whichever corner he took it on, in Winchester Fives it does, for he has the buttress to consider. If he chooses to strike on the left-hand side, he at once reduces the number of alternatives he has for the placing of his first cut. And then again, in Rugby Fives, only the server may take the striker's return of service, but in this game, either the server or his partner may take it, and it is generally the latter.

The striker has now an extra shot to utilize ; he can aim at the buttress. He may do this only in doubles. For if in singles he should strike the buttress full pitch with his first cut, it will count a let, because the server must be allowed a chance of reaching it. Even in doubles he will not make use of this stroke too often, especially if he is playing against a server who crouches under the buttress, but for the most part he will hit low and hard for the back left-hand corner, or the middle of the left-hand side wall, making quite sure that the server, should he be standing up, does not get an opportunity to volley his return. The server, after he has thrown the ball up, can do one of three things. He can crouch under the front wall, he can move to the centre of the court and hope to volley the striker's return, but thus unsighting his partner and giving him but a poor chance to return the ball, if he himself should miss it ; or he can stay on the right-hand side of the court, from where he has thrown the ball up, which will afford his partner a good sight of the ball and plenty of time to make his stroke, but will leave the buttress unguarded. We have discussed the various situations when the various positions are best taken up. There is no hard-and-fast rule, and a good pair might well use all three movements in the course of a game.

What are the advantages of a court with a buttress such as this over the court that has none ? It does of course lend an added interest to the game by presenting a goal for all who would test their accuracy and skill, and it does this, without becoming an absolute hazard like the ' pepper ' and ledges of an Eton Fives court. It brings an element of chance and the unexpected into the game, which is always dear to the heart of the spectator if not to the player. But it loses freedom thereby and it is the joy of hitting a ball around a confined space without fear of hazard that appeals to a man in Rugby Fives. There is nothing to be gained by a comparison between such games ; there are sports like golf and Eton Fives with known hazards of bunkers and buttresses, and there are sports that have none of these things ; they are both enjoyable, but their pleasure is not akin. Winchester Fives is like an attempt to find the happy medium between the games of Eton and Rugby, and in some odd way it succeeds. As it is played, the doubles game is most attractive, energetic and amusing, but a single is spoilt by the ease with which one may win a point.

It matters little whether you play Winchester Fives or Rugby Fives ; it matters a great deal that there are so few courts other than those to be found at schools and in University towns. In the whole of London, there is no convenient court where a man can get a game for a small fee. He must belong to a club

before he can play, a club for which he is not eligible. It is
claimed by those who have the money, and they are few to-day,
that it is unwise to run to the expense of building public courts,
because it is such a very young man's game. It is true that it
does demand much bending which the over thirty do not relish
and the over forty shrink from—and that is a reason, to be
ungallant for a moment, why it is not an entirely satisfactory
game for women—but that is no justification for their ceasing
to play, rather is it a motive for them to persevere. Whatever
is lost in speed and agility with the passing of years is more than
recompensed by the increased accuracy and craft which is the
fruit of long experience. This Dr. Cyriax and his friends have
ably proved, a lesson that some of us have learnt to our cost.

Fives has never been really popular and it will never be so,
for it is not spectacular. It has not the grace nor the elegance
of games played with a racket, nor the excitement of an outdoor
field game, but to play it is the greatest fun of all, because it
combines so admirably the best exercise with the right amount
of enthusiasm. All over the world it is known under different
names. In America, it is hand-ball ; in France, Jeu de Paume ;
in Spain, pelota—the very word means ball—and in England
Fives. As a game it is not national, but universal.

Printed in the USA
CPSIA information can be obtained
at www.ICGtesting.com
LVHW041833051023
760086LV00059B/1508